Keep t

LIFE AFTER DIVORCE

*The story of one pastor's triumph over
the tragedy of divorce*

Clinton McFarland

xulon PRESS

Life After Divorce
The Story of one Pastor's Triumph over the Tragedy of Divorce
by Rev. Clinton McFarland

Printed in the United States of America

ISBN 9781613793299

Unless otherwise indicated, Bible quotations are taken from The King James Version of the Bible. Copyright © 2000 by Zondervan; and The New American Standard Bible. Copyright ©1995 by Foundation Publications.

www.xulonpress.com

Dedication

I affectionately dedicate this book to those who have experienced the trauma of divorce. My prayer is that in some tangible way this book will provide a glimpse of the redeeming possibilities that can occur even after divorce.

ACKNOWLEDGEMENTS

First and foremost, I thank God for His marvelous mercy and sustaining presence which comforted me as I navigated through a painful chapter in my life. In reflection upon a once dismal valley, I am reminded that He remained faithfully present as I moved day by day. I am yet encouraged and acknowledge that He has not left me for a single moment.

I am eternally grateful to have been disciplined and directed by wonderful parents, The Reverend Cleveland and Dora McFarland. Adding to God's goodness, I was blessed with four stunning sisters; Patricia, Wenda, Sherry and Victoria, and three amazing brothers; Cleveland, Jr., Kenneth and Terry who played a major part in my becoming the man I am today. I thank God for all of you!

I am equally appreciative to God for my supportive wife and best friend, Tamara McFarland, whom I love with an inexpressible and indescribable love. There are no words sufficient enough to convey how much your presence in my life has helped me.

My heart beams with great pride as I thank my darling children, Dwanna and Clinton. Their existence has been an ultimate source of motivation and elation. I am proud to be the father of such wonderful offspring. My love for them in itself was enough to cause me to hold on and not give up. Thank you Dwanna and Clinton for giving me purpose.

My life and ministry has been shaped by the privilege to serve three progressive and challenging churches. I am eternally thankful for John the Baptist Church for having the confidence to call me to serve as their pastor. Secondly, I am most grateful to the Southside Missionary Baptist Church which stood with me and loved me back to health during a very trying time in my life. Thirdly, I am thankful to the marvelous congregation of Mt. Pleasant Missionary Baptist Church in Atlanta, Georgia where I currently serve as senior pastor at the time of this writing. I appreciate your trust in my leadership, support of the ministry, and expressions of love. I must extend special thanks to my staff for keeping me balanced. Thanks to Lynn Sorrell for your input in this project. God bless you Ronald Harbin, my true friend for over two decades. Thanks to both of you for friendship.

Table of Contents

Foreword xiii

Introduction xvii

The Leprosy Syndrome 27

The Blame Game 40

Smitten From the Very Beginning 57

The Beginning of the End 69

A Dead Man Preaching 85

An Emotional Roller Coaster 101

A Series of Aftershocks 116

Trusting God 136

How Does the Bible Address Divorce? 156

Try! Try Again! 180

New Mercies 201

Before You Leap! 230

Rise and Be Healed! 259

Epilogue

Settling the Matter 281

Foreword

(SUNRISE OVER A DARK HORIZON)
By Dr. Jamal Harrison Bryant

Most often, the very mention of divorce elicits negative sensations and sentiments. For many, the excruciating pain of divorce denotes failure, rejection, betrayal and hardship. As difficult as it is to face, we must admit in our culture we encounter this single occurrence with great frequency. Countless individuals are locked in a virtual emotional prison of guilt and shame over a failed marriage. As much as we would like to seek foolproof protection, neither socio-economic status, race or position can guarantee immunity from its prevailing statistics.

As a casualty of this painful wrecking experience, taking ownership and confronting my turbulent emotions, gave me permission to cry sometimes and in the process orchestrated the fulfillment of the very purpose for my sanity. Every ingredient I needed to master and move on has been insightfully pre-tested and proven in these pages to lend authenticity and empathy to what would otherwise be an abstract philosophy.

This book is equipped with classic substance for anyone to feed on the very stuff that survivors are made of. The Body of Christ still holds fast to the sacred and significant premise of forgiveness and restoration. The presence of pending divorce becomes an instance where sometimes we must come sadly before God and admit that once again, as in other matters, we have managed to fall short of His perfect will. It is for that reason, having treaded this tumultuous road, nationally renowned pastor and evangelist Rev. Clinton McFarland shares a very personal and painful journey as he addresses the issue head on.

In the role of a pastor and counselor, Rev. McFarland becomes quite transparent and approaches the entire matter from both biblical and human perspective. He provides rare insight and practical application through the thought and prayer processes necessary to survive the disconcerting circumstances so common with divorce. Step by step, he has developed a "recovery" plan as one faces perhaps the most devastating experience in life. More importantly, he brings a message of hope and redemption.

LIFE AFTER DIVORCE is a title whose time has come! It is a lifesaver for many—married, single, pastors, counselors and the general population. You have a choice to either spend years in therapy or sit down and absorb the insights that shine a bright light on the path toward reclaiming your spirit. Revisiting Clinton McFarland's journey will help many individuals transcend a dark horizon and emerge on the other side with a bright sunrise.

Rev/Dr. Jamal Harrison Bryant

Founder/Pastor,

Empowerment Temple, Baltimore Maryland

Introduction

There are many individuals who believe that I have committed a great offense. This is especially true among those who hold to the most traditional tenets of Christian doctrine. In their eyes, I have gone against the Word of God and deserve merciless scrutiny. In spite of any defense presented to this particular group, I probably emerge with, at best, diminished credibility. You see, I received a call by God to preach His Gospel. I answered that call. I met a beautiful young lady. I fell in love and married her. Next, I became the pastor of a congregation. Years later, I went through a DIVORCE!

I clearly understand that there are many who have already formed opinions of me because of this apparent transgression. They developed this opinion possibly because of how they feel about divorce or strictly because of the position that I hold within the community of Christendom.

I am not sure that I can ever change the unrelenting mindset of anyone who would toss the Scriptures at me and taunt me with this transgression; however, there are countless individuals in the Body of Christ who are locked in a virtual emotional prison because of guilt and shame over a failed marriage. I believe that there is liberation for you. There are other individuals who have yet to enter a marriage relationship who deserve a first-hand account of some of the factors, which present fatal hazards. It is my desire to provide an opportunity to better analyze the complexities in human relationships, especially as it relates to marriage and the unfortunate dissolution of marriage.

My life profile includes divorce. I am definitely not proud of this fact, and I will be forced to live with the repercussions of a family unit having been torn apart for the rest of my life. As a result of this, much has transpired in my life.

Initially, there were periods of loneliness far too difficult to verbalize. The displacement was agonizing. To this day there are times when I miss so much the opportunity to live in the same house with my children who are teen-agers at the time of this writing. You will comprehend this more as you read this book. You will see how the breaking of this holy union not only affected me but the beautiful children who were involved. It is just now that I am able to begin to share the nightmare of a broken home.

Rather than being there in the mix of things, I have often had to settle for an after-account of a special event in their lives instead of experiencing it firsthand. Sometimes, a digital photo has substituted for my actual presence to witness the event. In a perfect world, I should have been there. In a world of actuality, I no longer enjoy this unre-stricted privilege. I do make every effort to spend as much time as possible with my children. I am big on fatherhood. I am there for their mother to lend a helping hand, when needed. As a man and as a pastor, I am acutely aware of my role as a parent. As a child of the King, I also understand what is required of me in this area. In addition to a deep emotional attachment, I have fully honored my financial responsibility to take care of my children and their mother.

Even though I did not initiate divorce proceedings, I would have been less than a man to neglect my family or lower their standard of living. I could not have called myself a leader of God's people if I left my own family without adequate resources and reasonable protection. The Scripture teaches that a man who does not provide for his own is worst than an unbeliever.

Even in this valley-kind-of situation, God continues to claim glory in my life if no more than through my testimony and my WILLINGNESS to become TRANSPARENT in personal failures so that others might become blessed and over-comers in that same area. This book is MY TESTIMONY! Among other accomplishments for which I am eternally grateful, I now consider myself SUPER QUALIFIED to address marriage, divorce, male/female relationships and a host of family-related issues. My preparedness would not be as concentrated and on-point had I not gone through a very difficult and trying period in my life. My experience goes far beyond an "in theory only" saga.

Marriage is a fundamental building block of healthy communities and strong family units. In spite of its significance, every marriage has potential problems because the relationship involves people who are only human. Every personality, in spite of a possible illusion of perfection, will eventually reveal some faults.

Little did I know at the time of my marriage that it was one of the most difficult relationships to try to maintain successfully. We now live in a society where almost 60% of all marriages end up in divorce. In subsequent marriages for the second or third time, the statistics are far more alarming. Unfortunately, Christian marriages are subject to the same attack. Remember, my former wife and I are both Christians and it happened to us. Had anyone told me during our courtship and early marriage that we would one day dissolve this union, I would have told them they were crazy. A divorce, NOT ME! NOT IN MY HOME! NEVER!

Hopefully, reading this book will motivate those of you who are married to look closely at your situation, evaluate the circumstances, take full survey of the responsibilities, and then follow the godly steps necessary in dealing with any problem plaguing your relationship. This is most important because strong marriages make strong families. They are the beginning of the cycle, which builds or destroys entire communities. Optimally, when a mom and dad are on the same page then the lives of their children will more likely fall in place. The strength of a good marriage encourages the entire household to align with the perfect will of God.

The strength of a family is predicated upon the man and the woman playing the roles that God has assigned to them. According to biblical teaching, the husband is the HEAD of the house. The wife is the HEART of the house. Both are equally important; yet, their roles are uniquely different. Both individuals bring a different set of needs and sensitivities as a human being into the marriage as well. When these needs are reassigned, compromised, stifled, ignored or misunderstood there is usually trouble down the road. Sometimes these troubles are minor and can be easily repaired. The signals may be a little difficult to discern in the very beginning. At other times they are blatant and significant enough to shatter the foundation of the relationship. Ignoring these signs contributes greatly to the staggering 60% divorce rate mentioned earlier. By the way, according to a recent Barna survey, over 15% of the marriages of Christian pastors end in divorce. I wish there was a way to discover how many couples in ministry are contemplating divorce right now. I have a feeling the numbers are shocking or at least much higher than 15%. I have chosen to isolate statistics in the lives of clergy because firstly, I am a member of that segment of the population and I interact with so many pastors. Secondly, I am painfully aware that other people watch us and are both positively and negatively influenced by our living example.

I also have a compelling desire to reach individuals who have never entered into a marital covenant. Understanding God's full intent and purpose for marriage will help you to build a secure and healthier relationship. There are blessings in waiting patiently on Him before entering into what He designed originally as a lifelong commitment. There are additional blessings to be had in seeking His face and submitting to pre-marital counseling through a church, a pastor or a Christian organization certified to provide such services. If Mr. or Mrs. "Right" has knocked you off of your feet and you are thinking of marriage, then make sure that you find someone to help you. As they say, "Love is blind." However, I can assure you it does not take long after entering a marriage that your vision becomes sharp and clear. The blindness strangely disappears. You may even wish to be blind again! Wouldn't you rather have 20/20 vision going into the marriage rather than two or three years down the road; or worse, two or three WEEKS down the road?

Then, there are the marriages of clergy, many of which are in deep trouble. Be assured, if it happened to me, it can happen to you. Don't make the mistakes openly confessed in this book. Don't become so heavenly-minded that you overlook earthly responsibilities. Someone once said, "There is no excuse for tremendous public success and private failure at home."

During my divorce, I had to make sure that my congregation understood that marriage remains GOD'S idea and represents one of the sweetest blessings He affords to us as followers. I did not want the church to experience a wave of divorces with more men than usual walking out on their families. This was already a problem in our communities. Likewise, I did not want the women in the congregation to start announcing that they had had enough and did not want their husbands anymore! I have heard of this happening within congregations after the leader's home was torn apart.

When both of us acknowledged that we were at a point of impasse and I finally accepted the fact that my former wife, in spite of my willingness and pleas to reconcile, was not going to change her mind, we went together before the congregation and announced that we were ending the marriage. It was a sad day for all of us.

Some members of the congregation were not so surprised because I had been under great duress for quite some time. Others were shocked. In spite of the reaction, as a body, they were concerned and mourned with us.

As you read this account of my life, I pray that you will accept my transparency understanding that it reflects my personality. I believe that the only way I can help people with my experience is to be as open and honest as I can. It is not my desire to merely share my saga with you, but to use it to encourage others who have experienced this difficult ordeal. The difficulty of it is inexpressible, but there is good news; just as God helped and healed me, He can do the same for you.

It is my endeavor to offer HELP for the helpless and HOPE for the hopeless. You will find this AND MORE in my personal account.

Chapter One

THE LEPROSY SYNDROME

In the book of Mark, we find an account of the plight of several individuals afflicted with leprosy. This was a terrible and dreaded disease, which could not be cured by the physicians of that day. It was impossible to hide the disease because its symptoms were obvious and gross. The skin became scaly and irritated. There were boils which oozed with an unsightly flow of pus. No one wanted to be near a person with this condition. The lepers then were banished from their homes to live together in a colony or sub-community. Generally, people believed that some great sin had been committed which brought about this life of misery. Sometimes they even assumed that the lepers' parents were responsible and had sinned to the point that their offspring had been cursed. Lepers were also not allowed to go into the temple as others worshipped. Putting it mildly, they were outcasts!

When walking through the town or village they were required to cry out, "Unclean, Unclean!" This cry served as a warning to anyone in close proximity to stay at a safe distance or risk being contaminated. Can you just imagine how it must have felt to go down the street, ashamed of your appearance and indicted by the words coming from your own mouth?

The progression of the disease involved the numbing of nerve endings to the point that the afflicted person eventually experienced no sensation of touch or feel. In the latter stages, it often caused portions of the body, especially toes and fingers, to separate or self-amputate from the body. It was one of the most unsightly diseases a person could have.

The comparison may seem a little extreme; however, there are conditions and circumstances that can come into our lives which are capable of placing us in emotional isolation and shame. Because of the way some people might react or treat us, we may feel banished and tossed aside. One of these situations involves trying to overcome the stigma of divorce—especially if you are a Christian! It is even worse if you are a pastor. Remember, there are some folk who still believe that once divorced an individual must be SENTENCED to a life of singleness, loneliness and unworthiness. However, I strongly disagree.

It is heartbreaking that divorcees are sometimes received with such caution. This is the time that we need caring and compassionate people in our lives When people start to treat you like you are diseased or contaminated it plays a psychological game with your mind. After a while we begin to suspect ourselves. Inexorably, when treated a certain way, sometimes we begin to view ourselves as others perceive us.

I have known people who have gone into deep depression triggered by reactions from other individuals particularly when they have experienced a traumatic situation. And of course, there is nothing more traumatizing than the tearing away of the person you most deeply love. This happened to me. I started wondering – is there something really wrong with me? Am I as bad as some would suggest but am unaware of it? These become real thoughts when you are categorized as a leper.

I can remember several individuals whom I considered as fairly good friends and ministry comrades who immediately kicked me to the curb after learning that my marriage was in trouble. They no longer wanted to associate with me or considered me suitable for remaining within their circle of friends. I had to deal with not only the loss of the woman whom I loved, my children and my standard of life, but I also lost associates whom I thought would aid me through the process. Not only did this surprise me, it also hurt! I can only imagine how the lepers felt.

Even though afflicted, hurt and bewildered, I was not ready to declare myself "unclean." I CERTAINLY did not have any plans to remove myself from the Temple (God's House). If nobody else knew, then I was certain that God was aware of how painful and difficult this whole matter had become. I share this because there are some denominations that mandate that the pastor be relieved of his pastoral duties if he goes through a divorce. This is true regardless of the circumstances which caused the proceedings. There are no questions asked. You are divorced! You are a leper! Goodbye and good riddance!

This is true not only for those of us who are a part of the clergy community. I have come into contact with many whom, because of the failure of their marriages, were treated with caution. One person in particular comes to mind who was dismissed from his duties in a very prestigious religious organization. Many people whom he and his wife associated with at social gatherings severed their relationships with him. I remember talking to him about it and noted how devastated he had become as a result of this insensitive treatment. I guess some of his colleagues felt that divorce was contagious or he had committed blasphemy or some unforgivable sin.

Personally, I had to deal with all of the fabricated accusations that circulated in regards to the breakup of my marriage. Of course, everyone had his or her own opinion as to the rationale behind it. It's kind of funny now as I reflect upon some of the hilarious stories that were told, but believe me, it was not funny then. I would often sit and wonder why people would automatically think that I was in this situation because of something evil that I had done. I must say that this is particularly true especially for a man of means and position. We are constantly under suspicion and scrutiny.

I recall one incident that occurred as I was in the grocery store. I ran into a person whom I knew well. I tried to get his attention so that I could speak to him. In the beginning, he acted as if he did not know me. When I finally got his attention, he spoke to me as if I was diseased. I still remember the pain that I felt. I had now experienced rejection simply because I was divorced. It is so amazing to me how people can stick to you like glue when you are up and later shun you as though you carry a fatal plague.

Not only did I have to deal with those who were bitter because I was perceived as a poor representation of Christ, but I also had some supporters. The only problem was that even the supporters actually believed some of those outlandish stories. They would approach me in a different way. Surprisingly, they were willing to forgive me for stuff that I did not know that I had done! I remember one person saying to me, "Pastor, I still love you and support you because everybody makes mistakes, and you are a man just like every other man." Those were some difficult times.

Believe me when I say that I certainly was not beyond reproach in my marriage and in my life. Romans 3:23 certainly applies to me—"All have sinned and come short of the glory of God"—but it's an awful feeling when people are accusing and forgiving you for stuff that you are certain you did not do! Since you are divorced, from their perspective, you obviously had to do what they said you did.

What I really like about Mark's account of the story of the lepers is that one of them had the foresight to take his problem directly to Jesus. He found the strength to approach the Master and uttered the life-changing plea, *"If thou will, make me clean!"*

You see, in my heart I approached Jesus in a similar manner. I poured out my heart, bowed before Him and asked Him to consider me in the midst of a mess—one that I admit I had partially brought upon myself. Again, I must admit that I was not innocent in the marriage but like that leper, I asked Him to make me clean. I already knew it was His will. From the moment that I began to study the Bible as a child, all that I read taught me that His promises remained "Yea" and "Amen."

I was even more blessed as I read these words:

"AND JESUS MOVED WITH COMPASSION AND SAID, BE THOU CLEAN!"

The most significant word here is **"compassion."** During the worst of this personal trial I was forced to ask myself, "Where is compassion when things just happen, and we can't fix it the way people want?" I have never been able to see why people who claim to be followers of Christ cannot exemplify the COMPASSION of Christ. All through the Scriptures we see how Jesus handled his followers with compassion, sympathy, and empathy.

I read about a woman caught in the very act of adultery. Her accusers eventually brought her to Jesus. I paid careful attention to how Jesus so graciously handled the situation. He stooped and began writing something on the ground. He then looked up and said to her accusers, "He that is without sin, let him cast the first stone." He then looked at the woman after the departure of her accusers and said, "Where are your accusers? Didn't one of them condemn you?"

"No, Lord," she said.

Jesus said, "Neither do I. Go, and sin NO MORE!"

My God, what compassion! He didn't shun her or kick her while she was down and already hurting. Rather, He showed her that He loved her in spite of her obvious transgression.

I encourage you to not allow the failure of a relationship or marriage result in your leprosy. Don't allow anyone to force you to wear an invisible sign which reads "UNCLEAN!" You may have siblings who managed to avoid going through the ending of a marriage. As a result, you may feel you are a lesser person. Jesus washed your condition away on Calvary. He did it in advance so that you would not have to be condemned.

We often quote John 3:16 but the message of redemption is really more evident in John 3:17.

"For God sent NOT His Son into the world to condemn the world but that the world through Him might be saved."

In other words, God, in His infinite mercy, has not closed the doors of heaven to divorcees or to any other person who temporarily falters or may fall victim to unfortunate circumstances. We fall down but GET BACK UP! Psalm 37:23-24 says, *"The steps of a good man are ordered by the LORD: and he delights in his way. THOUGH HE FALLS, he shall not be utterly cast down: for the LORD upholds him with his hand."*

Think about the occurrence of accidents; there are those which happen TO us and those which we may cause. The insurance industry handled it adequately when they introduced the "no fault" status. Even if, in the eyes of your friends and family, it initially seemed to be your fault, Jesus has paid it all!

I certainly do not mean to create a haven of escape for individuals who would willfully dishonor marriage and distort its Holiness and prominence in God's plan for human relationships. However, I want to open a door to freedom for individuals who have been living under a virtual cloud because families, society, and unfortunately, the Body of Christ have condemned them and cast them away.

Please allow me to share a sad but true story:

There was a couple with several young children. The wife connected with a fundamentalist church whose leader admonished her to live apart from her husband because he was not saved. She felt as though she would have been in sin living with her husband and defying the words of her pastor. (She had not been a member of the church when they married). After joining she felt she was in error marrying a man who did not meet the requirements of the doctrine of her church and leader. She spent a lifetime making amends and apologizing for this "mistake." By the way, this same leader did not condone divorce.

The mother and her young children lived in a separate residence away from her husband for years. He provided for them, paid the rent, saw the children through elementary school and then through college. For decades, this couple lived apart. The husband carried the expense of both households. Later, all the children were grown and their parents still lived apart.

After many years, the mother died. She had loved her husband all of these years, and he had loved her. Both had been locked in a prison of legalism. Neither had enjoyed a full life. The husband was so distraught at her death that he could not attend the home going service. I am not suggesting that the couple should have gotten a divorce. If they were able to dwell together peaceably, I feel they should have remained together—without interference! Who knows, one day he might have joined the church. However, who can blame him for not wanting to connect to the very institution that he perceived as the destroyer of his home. This is only one tragic example of how others can use the Bible to inflict ridiculous restrictions and regulations upon our lives. Every single situation is unique and worthy of God's direction and wisdom.

Wouldn't it be nice if the church would embrace the real essence of Christianity? It is more detrimental to the body of Christ when we display our judgmental attitudes because we perceive someone to be a leper or unclean. We do more to stop the expansion of the church by how we treat those who have fallen prey to some seemingly unpardonable offense. Whatever happened to Galatians 6:1 which states, *"Brothers, if someone is caught in a sin, you who are SPIRITUAL should restore him gently? But watch yourself, or you also may be tempted"?*

I am a part of a local church and certainly I don't want to cast a shadow of negativity on the church, but unfortunately it is an army that will sometimes kill her already wounded soldiers. Certainly, this is not God's desire for how we should function. His desire is that we are merciful. Jesus said in what is called the Sermon on the Mount that it is the **merciful who will obtain mercy**.

Are you going through life with your head down? Does your self-esteem and interaction with others cry out that you are "unclean?" As of this day, I encourage you to **CHOOSE NOT TO BE A LEPER. YOU CAN BE CLEAN AND WHOLE AGAIN!**

Let's continue this journey together!

Chapter Two

THE BLAME GAME

When we ask the question, who is to blame, of course both members of the marriage should stop and take a look in the mirror. I am a firm believer that it is not the apple on the tree that causes us harm; rather, it is the PAIR on the ground. You may not understand clearly what I am saying, but I am thinking in terms of the first couple –Adam and Eve. When they experienced negative consequences as a result of their ways of transgressions, they failed to take personal responsibility. Shockingly, they turned on each other. This is prevalent in marriages when upheaval arises.

God confronted the couple in the cool of the evening. It was then that Adam said, "Lord, this woman that you gave me persuaded me to break your commandment." Eve blamed the serpent. But when you read this account in its entirety, you will likely discover that it was not the apple on the tree but the PAIR that was on the ground—the man and the woman!

Most people believe the fruit to be an apple but the biblical account actually does not specify. I do not know if it was an apple or not, but I do know that when a couple deals with issues that are detrimental to their marriage it is true that it is not the fruit on the tree; rather it is the imperfect PAIR on the ground. This statement forces me to take full responsibility for those things that went wrong in MY life and marriage. I choose to do this. Actually, I believe that taking responsibility for what takes place in your life is a good thing. It is liberating. It is life- changing and imperative if you are going to move from where you are to where you endeavor to go. To make matters simple, we must look in the mirror!

There are those who think that accepting the blame or taking responsibility for a situation which involves another person involves letting the other person off of the hook. But to the contrary, it actually lets you off the hook because it frees you to move on. Remember that the title of this book is LIFE AFTER DIVORCE. Believe me when I tell you that you DO want life after the finalization of your divorce. One of the things that you can't do is embrace your future when you are chained to your past. Again I say, "We must look in the mirror!"

The death of Michael Jackson during the summer of 2009 immediately flooded the airways, one after the other, with his greatest hits. One recording-breaking selection which topped the charts was "Man in the Mirror." How could this possibly relate to me and the end of my marriage, or of any marriage?

Yes, there were some outside influences which contributed greatly to the decay and demise of our marriage relationship. I will be deliberately cautious as to how much I expound upon that because it is not my intention to indict anyone. More importantly, in retrospect after the divorce, I was forced not only to look at my former wife's unwillingness to remain in the marriage, but at my own failures as well. I finally stood in the mirror. This time I saw stains and flaws that I had never faced before.

It is amazing what is revealed when we look in the mirror. I did it and the person I saw was—ME? Wow!

What I saw was revealing and startling. I certainly saw a brother who thought that he had it all together. But, actually he was UNDONE. Let me really be honest. Prior to this set of circumstances I had a view of myself through the selected best photographs of life versus the real mirror of life. This is the mistake that so many of us make not understanding that there is a difference between the image from a photograph and the image in the mirror.

Photography is really an art form. A professional can adjust the light on one side and brighten the light on the other side. He can push the lens in or pull the lens out so that he might be creative in capturing an image. Nevertheless, when you look in the mirror, you will see YOU for who YOU really are. Oh, one more thing you will ascertain is that the mirror does not lie!

The question remains on the table: Who is to be blamed?

The answer will be predicated upon who's answering the question. The fact of the matter is that everybody does not view situations the same way. Most people describe situations through their own PARADIGM. What do I mean by paradigm? I simply mean a frame of reference. Everyone has a frame of reference through which they see life and life's circumstances. To break it down, your paradigm represents the information or experience by which you view a particular situation.

One can look at life and see sorrow while the other can look at life and see success. Through my eyes at that time, I probably perceived that my former wife played the greater part in the breakup of our marriage. In contrast to my perception, she (through her eyes) would probably believe that I contributed in greater part to the breakup of our marriage. That's just the way it is in life. This was probably one of the greatest contributors to the breakup of our marriage as I'm sure it is with most marriages. The fact is that we give blame but we can't take blame. I'm sure that if I could have seen things through her eyes and she through my eyes then we could have found resolution in the matter. At that time, neither of us was willing to stand and take that all-revealing look in the mirror.

That, of course, is not the easiest thing to do. It is because we are so caught up in our own paradigms until we don't have time or don't make time to consider the perception or need of others. It fits a basic definition of selfishness—an aggravating visitor in many marriages. And, selfish we were!

As a pastor, I have counseled with many couples who are dealing with problems in their marriage. They will come to me with their version of the problem. What I have continued to listen for but have never heard is a person who would say, "I know that if I considered the feelings of my spouse we could make this thing work." Instead, I have heard constant babbling concerning MY needs. "If SHE would do this" or "If HE would do that" then our marriage would work.

When we constantly blame others for our actions or inactivity it causes us to fail to look at the real problem. We are so busy looking out of the window when the problem is not out the window but in the mirror. Real resolution will come when BOTH persons take responsibility for what occurs in our life, but I must admit that both "blaming" and "accusing" found their way into my marriage. I think about it now and feel that I should have known better. I have counseled many couples and have watched how destructive this kind of behavior is to a relationship; yet I, fire-baptized and full-of-the-Gospel, fell prey. What I have now learned is that it is extremely hazardous when we get caught up in our own selfishness.

I have often wondered why I was able to see all of this about myself after the failure of the relationship but couldn't see it then. I guess it was because I was in the fire and found it a lot easier to inspect her rather than inspect myself. I think about it now in hindsight. You know what they say about hindsight. I'm talking about that 20/20 vision that I earlier shared with you.

At one point we went to marriage counseling, and it was disastrous. I am almost ashamed to admit that we totally dumbfounded the counselor with our selfishness and fault- finding in everyone but ourselves. The counselor was amazed. We were a special case. One thing that did happen as a result of counseling was that things emerged that we didn't know were there.

I'm almost reluctant to address this issue because it can get kind of sticky. I am making every effort to not let it get that way. If I go any deeper into those counseling sessions I would embarrass myself. Just believe me, it was a mess! Here I was pointing at her when there were three fingers pointing back at me. I want to make sure that I don't repeat the finger pointing in this book. So for the sake of avoiding it I accept responsibility for what I did wrong. That's the point we must get to. Even though I'm willing to take personal responsibility, I do understand that the "PAIR PRINCIPLE" is still prevalent.

It takes Two

To answer my own question, factually **both of us were to blame.** That's the truth! Whenever you have the breakup of a marriage then it is the fault of both parties. I'll say it again, "it takes two to argue." This is what I believe couples should know. It takes two to make it work and two to tear it up. I am aware of the fact that there are times when you happen to hook up with a person who is just a plain idiot and he or she just does not care about their marriage or anything else. Thank God that was not our case.

When we met and married, I believe that we both tried very hard to make a great marriage and a wonderful family. We were not idiots who just didn't care, but we were people who still must take blame for our marital demise. We were not mean but just green. She did some things wrong, and I can write a whole chapter on the things that I did wrong.

47

Now I know that whenever an agreement or covenant is broken, there is still a natural tendency to transfer the blame. I am glad that this did not start with me and my ex-wife. Actually, it started with the first couple brought together by God.

Let's revisit "The Blame Game" as played by Adam and Eve:

(1) Adam: "Lord, this woman that you gave to me is the reason I'm in this mess. If you had not insisted that it was not good for me to be alone I would not have to deal with the punishment that I'm receiving."

(2) Eve: "Lord, this snake tricked me. I was beguiled by this snake and that's the reason I broke your rules."

Now back to my situation. I know that it takes two to mess it up but this is my book and my opportunity to vent, come clean and confess. Before you get too happy, don't think that I'm getting ready to spill my guts. Even though at times I'll be somewhat transparent, this is not meant to be a "tell-all" literary encounter which goes into the intricate details of my relationship. We have heard about a lot of these accounts in recent years—from politicians, celebrities, and athletes. There have also been some rather over-publicized accounts of breakups and among well-known nationally recognized preachers and spiritual leaders. In many instances, they were the victims of over-zealous media attention.

Sensationalism has never been my goal. Personal deliverance and emotional healing of others is at the top of my agenda. Thus, we have the rationale for my writing this book. I carry a burden for anyone who needs spiritual direction in a difficult situation, especially in a divorce.

If we are honest, the more we examine the end of a relationship as serious as marriage, the more we are forced to confess human faults and error. It is sometimes difficult and extremely painful to face the whole truth. The ability to confess opens the door to emotional and spiritual freedom. The absence of this same ability can delude one into denying responsibility and contributions to a situation which might not have occurred otherwise.

The act of confession provides the opportunity to be straightforward and cleanse oneself of guilt and burdens.

Many times it brings healthy resolution and peace. Try it as you deal with your situation – be it divorce or something else. I'm certainly not saying that you have to write a book about your personal failures but being honest with yourself, God, and even the other person involved can be quite invigorating.

The last months of our marriage were quite difficult for me. The difficulty was so acute because, in spite of everything that I tried to do to rekindle the love and affection at home, it felt as though I ran into a concrete wall.

I could dwell on the fact that she no longer wanted me, but I would do better to look at the things that I did to make her not want me. In retrospect, there are many things that I could have done differently. Of course, this may not be your situation. You may not have done anything wrong; but I did.

Most marriage counselors concur that there is blame on both sides in the demise of a marriage. Generally, they indicate that no one person can be totally at fault. As for me, I'd rather take the high (honest) road and confess personal error. Therefore, I take full responsibility for not recognizing the symptoms of a marriage on life-support. Even though she asked OUT of the marriage, I must assume responsibility for its ultimate death. You see, in biblical terms, I was the PRIEST of our home and relationship. It was my duty to provide, protect, cherish, and fortify the marriage. As with most individuals, I was better at some facets of priesthood than others. I did try to fix multiple problems but my efforts were too late into the game. In an emotional sense, the other player had vacated the court. I could not play alone. Perhaps I unknowingly drove her emotions and affection away. Maybe, there were too many times when I should have been on the court at playing time and I failed to appear.

Now, I see a series of things that I did wrong or could have done better. This was important for me to come to terms with. My marriage did not come to this point overnight. There were continuous transgressions and mistakes on my part; probably from the very beginning. **Please understand, dear reader, that when a couple breaks up it is not the result of a blowout but more likely, a slow leak.** It's like a car tire that goes flat and is no longer operable. Some tires blow out all of a sudden while others just have a slow leak that goes unnoticed until it's totally flat. That's what happened in my marriage.

My slow leak, the thing that I will confess is that things were taking place all around me and I was too wrapped up in my own world to notice them early on. One of the major causes of marriages being dissolved is not because of the wrong that is done but because we are blind to what is happening and never attempt to do anything about it. Before we know it, it's too late. The situation has gone too far and has lacked attention far too long.

Let's talk about another slow leak in marriage – not being careful with our words. Words are like water running from a faucet. Once they come out you cannot push them back. Many marriages are torn apart because of what we constantly say or don't say to our spouse. Words, words, words! One person so erroneously stated that "sticks and stones may break my bones but words will never harm me." That's a lie! **Words will not only harm you but can cause a slow and agonizing death.**

Were there unfortunate or regrettable words said? Yes, there were; and not only were there words spoken, but there were words unspoken. I'm talking about the failure to accentuate the positive. What do I mean by this? There were times when I missed the opportunity to highlight the good. I didn't fail at this on purpose but it happened. All of this contributed to the slow leak.

All right! I take the blame and she takes the blame, but I must share with you the fact that there were other countering forces working against us as well. I promise you that when I say this I am not trying to use a scapegoat or pass the blame; but there are some times other people and forces that we allow into our marriage which will then cause that godly union to dissolve. Still, that does not erase the things that I did or failed to do to avoid the ending of the bond with my ex-wife. Believe me when I tell you that there is more blame to go around.

This is a message to those who are married or contemplating marriage. In order for marriage to work, it is imperative that we eliminate any force which seeks to destroy your marriage intentionally or unintentionally. This will give your marriage a much greater chance of avoiding disaster.

Our problems were enhanced by outside intervention and ill-advised opinions from external sources. These external sources hurt the marriage in irreconcilable ways. A marriage can have its problems and make it as long as the problem stays within the home and marriage. The problem is compounded when we invite others into the equation. A couple can argue at home and in private and after it is over they can make up and move on. It is when others become aware of the situation, particularly in a non-professional capacity, where the marriage falls into jeopardy. Mature individuals must also stand in the mirror and ask themselves, "Why did we let these people into our lives and personal affairs?"

I will not deal with this much because again, it is not my attempt to indict anyone, especially when WE allowed these forces to infiltrate the union.

1 John 1:9 states that "If you confess your sins, God is faithful and just to forgive you of your sins and cleanse you from all unrighteousness."

I believe that these are personal and private matters in spite of the fact there might have been wrongs committed. Whatever my former wife did that I perceived as wrong is over and done with. By the same token, whatever I did is now over. I have confessed at least as much as I can. I am not confessing to the priest. I am not confessing to the church, but I have been very careful to confess my short-comings to God and to my former wife. This is what the Bible requires in order to receive forgiveness. You see, not confessing weakness can lead to wickedness! Had I known better I would have most likely done a lot better at being the husband I should have been.

In the words of an iconic Apostle Paul, "Forgetting those things that are behind and reaching forth to those things that are before." In other words, these are moments that we cannot regain or relive. Complete revelation of the events will not change a thing. My family suffered a devastating and painful experience. It is not necessary to divulge every tidbit of dissension or create a scoreboard which publicly displays our individual shortcomings. This is not a game of darts. The question is how can admis-sion of such failure help the countless individuals that will eventually read this book? How can our pain reduce your pain? What is the message God has for us as we enter into relationship with another person?

These are the questions that I have tried to answer and concerns that I've made an attempt to address. I no longer want to play THE BLAME GAME. It's too painful. It's too costly. It's unhealthy. The real truth is that nobody wins!

Chapter Three

SMITTEN FROM THE VERY BEGINNING

I don't laugh at people who claim that they fell in love at first sight. You see, it happened to me. I fell hopelessly in love with my former wife the moment I laid eyes on her! She was seventeen years old and I was twenty-one.

It was at the Wednesday night Bible class at my home church where my father was pastor when it all began. I didn't know her but I did notice her. She was breathtaking. She came with a guy whom she was dating, and I was there with the young lady whom I was dating. (We were always taught to bring our dates to Bible class).

She was there and MY GOD, I saw her! I must admit that I could not help but notice her beauty and was moved by her noticeable shyness. I know what you are thinking.

Didn't you say that you were there with your date? Yes I was, but since my mother taught me that an honest confession is just good for the soul; I must be honest. After that point I did not see anyone else in the room or hear anything that my father was teaching. I was SMITTEN!

Please understand that I only share this part of my life with you so that I might bring you (the reader) into my mental space.

When the relationship that I was involved in ended; I inquired about this mysterious lady. Since she was still in high school, I asked a friend about her. I also asked him to relay the effect that she had on me after our brief encounter. I was not sure if she noticed me or knew me, but I was going to make sure that if she didn't, that she would.

My friend did as I had asked and it was then that I discovered that the relationship with the guy that she was dating had come to an end as well. My, my I thought. Every man for himself and God for us all! I sent a message to her to see if I could call her. She consented. I called and we talked for a while but she seemed to be busy. I later discovered that she was just apprehensive about communicating with me. You see at that time I was, (what you might call) a "playa." She, I later discovered, was very much aware of that. After that brief telephone conversation, I decided to wait before I called her again.

As I was waiting, I received a phone call from her and it was absolutely on! We talked a lot and enjoyed very nice conversations. It wasn't long before I asked her to be my girl and we developed a very serious relationship.

This was a number of years ago when it was not so unusual for young people to develop more serious relationships and marry at an early age. Of course, things are much different now. However, after meeting this one, "Mr. Playa" had stopped in his tracks for all the right reasons. This was my catch for life; or so I thought.

I wasted no time entering an appropriate relationship. We dated and enjoyed what would today be considered as a rather "lame" courtship, but I was happy. She was the apple of my eye.

For many years, I had served as organist for my father. So, the preacher's musician had fallen in love with a sweet young woman. We dated for approximately a year and made plans to enter into holy matrimony.

Then, guess what? Approximately one month before our wedding, I accepted my call into the Gospel ministry. Oh yes, I fought it but by this time I was out of breath. I discovered that my arms were too short to box with God. God called ME from the KEYBOARD to the BOOK BOARD! Actually, the call had been on my life for years but I wanted to play the "Jonah role." I embarked upon the wrong ship headed in the wrong direction. In other words, I chose not to hear or follow. I chose to be "hearing-impaired" and pretended not to hear the call. I must confess that preaching and especially becoming a pastor was not on my life's agenda. You see, my father, brother, and uncle were preachers/pastors and I observed from a distance the difficulty they encountered. I just didn't want it. In fact, neither of us had planned on this preacher journey. I did learn one essential lesson: *God's ways are not our ways and His thoughts are not our thoughts.*

I had my fun as a single man. It was now time to settle down with one woman for life! The Scripture about marrying rather than "burning" indicated to me that I needed to change my circumstances. After all, I was first a preacher's kid and a Christian. There were certain societal expectancies that came along with that role. I wanted to be in full compliance not just with society but more importantly, WITH GOD!

We got married, but we had not factored this "ministerial dilemma" into our future relationship. This sudden shift was enough to challenge any young relationship. I felt that as the leader in the marriage that if she loved me then she would adjust to this new role. Unfortunately, it was not that easy for her. Equally unfortunate, even though sympathetic, I could not understand actually how tough this could be at the time. So, I proceeded to put more pressure on her to "get it together." I did try to offer help and to be patient. If being called to be a preacher wasn't enough, in a matter of months I was called to my first church in Pachuta, MS. Don't laugh, the word is pronounced "*Pa chu' ta*." This was another major adjustment for both of us.

The John the Baptist Church was my beloved. Things were going pretty well even with the challenges, although they were still prevalent. I was still smitten and still very much in love. Here we were now adjusting to this small church in rural Mississippi when, after seven years, I felt the call of God to leave there and accept the call to Southside Missionary Baptist, a larger church in Columbus, Mississippi. I was thrilled with this new opportunity. It represented an advance toward my goal to be used mightily and impact many souls for the Kingdom. Although, I was not thrilled initially about preaching the Gospel, after accepting I had now become very energetic and ambitious.

This certainly did not do much to enhance an already challenged marriage, but we persevered because I was still smitten and believed that she was too. The problem was that love was not enough to keep us together. I know what the song says, but love didn't keep us together. Love is a very important and essential element but it takes more than that. We were smitten and in love but were we compatible?

You can probably ask anyone who has been in a failed marriage and they will most likely agree that there were indisputable signs, which indicated some sort of incompatibility or potential serious discord down the road. Like many, I recognized these signs but did not know how to properly address them. Too often, couples marry in hopes of changing another person. This can result in a lifetime of conflict, needless hurt, and disappointment.

At the time of our marriage, I was twenty-two and she was eighteen. I had lived in other cities and had a chance to experience at least some degree of adult independence. In contrast, her realm of experience was limited and extremely sheltered. This was certainly not her fault. However, it contributed to a set of circumstances, which challenged our relationship and my then limited ability to cope.

I would describe my personality as that of an extrovert. I meet no strangers and will enter into conversation with someone I've never met and enjoy every moment. I tell jokes and enjoy laughter. It doesn't bother me if someone challenges my opinion or rejects my suggestion. I can hold my own.

In retrospect, I noticed that she exhibited characteristics, which to me indicated that she was perhaps an introvert. She seemingly did not feel at ease in strange surroundings and in interaction with lots of people. She continued to struggle with shyness. I made a note to work on this and help her to change. Big mistake on my part! I would have done better working on me or asking God to work on both of us and help us to find that "happy median" in the middle of the road called compatibility.

Remember, I had not accepted the call to ministry when I asked for her hand in marriage. It was not like we had any time while dating to see if her personality was compatible to my call. Maybe if I had been a preacher/pastor during the dating period I could have been more observant and possibly might have warned her about this kind of life. Possibly, she could have tested the waters herself to see if she was cut out for this, but we didn't have this privilege.

It was after a full year of dating that I dropped this bombshell. Prior to that time, I was on a crusade to convince God that in this one instance, He had the wrong man! I had been a "playa" in my day and had done practically every silly and mindless thing that occurs to a young man at this age. I was not an immoral person, but I sure wasn't trying to wear a clergy collar either. Oh no! Surely God did not want to use me! Well, as it turns out, God had decided to do just that. It really did not matter if I agreed with this designation or not. How did Minister Darryl Coley put it? "God is Sovereign. He can do whatever He wants to whenever He wants to." At this point, God was certainly all up in the middle of my plans. And, that's where He belonged—then and to this day! Ambassador Andrew Young once said, "If you want to make God laugh then just tell him your plans." I kept telling God my plans and evidently, He kept laughing.

My fiancée, who had once looked so forward to marrying her prince, had now become the wife of a Baptist preacher! This introduced another set of dynamics, which could have been problematic for any woman, especially someone so very young. In some settings, she would now be expected to function as the better half of a man of the cloth. She was a sweet, quiet picture of youth. She had not bargained for this SET APART life and the scrutiny and society-imposed standards, which unfortunately go along with being identified as the wife of a pastor.

In the beginning, more than once, I suggested that maybe we should wait to marry. It was certainly not because I wanted to but I thought that it might be better if we gave it some more time. I thought that we perhaps needed to grow some more. This hurt her tremendously. So, I did the "honorable" thing. I went ahead and met her at the altar. I trusted God to fix everything that caused me concern. After all, I loved this woman the very moment that I laid eyes on her. However, in the back of my mind, there were a lot of things that required fixing.

I want to be completely fair in describing our relationship. For the last few years of her childhood she grew up without her father. After we were married, I then unknowingly proceeded to assume the role somewhat of a father, which I admit, sometimes tried my patience. It wasn't a total bad experience because I actually enjoyed some of these times together. I taught her to drive a manual shift automobile and a number of other things that a woman would normally come into the marriage having already experienced at the hands of her father or after having left her parents home to live on her own.

I believe that she enjoyed this protection and would retreat somewhat when I would try to pull her to the forefront to assume a more assertive role in our relationship. I wanted her to be my wife and not my daughter. I'm certainly not suggesting that she was immature but there were times that I felt more like a father than a husband. A disturbing fallacy, which was painfully apparent to me at that point, was that emotionally my need for a real partnership was in a state of imbalance. I did not know how to fix it and eventually pretended that things were better than they were. That was my way of escape. I stuck my head into the sand, buried my emotions and ran on to preach the gospel. Having failed to address the gravity of the matter, neither of us was prepared to salvage a blissful dream going sour.

There were other noticeable early signs of differences in our personalities and preferences that I do not feel the need to address in this book. It is not necessary. Every couple coming together to form a union probably experiences this period of initial adjustment. I think that I have made my point.

Eventually, there were serious signs of problems in epic proportions. Economically, we were living well. We had material possessions and two beautiful children whom we both loved dearly. I was pastor of a good church with a fine congregation. The church was one of the leading congregations in the state. Yet, it was as though we were living a bad dream—the kind from which you would just like to wake up and discover that it is all better. Oh, how I wished! Unfortunately, it was not that easy for her. Equally unfortunate, even though sympathetic, I could not understand actually how tough this could be at the time. So, I proceeded to wait and hope and pray that we could get it together. Oh, I admit that at times I thought that I had it together only to fool myself.

Sometimes there are unseen hazards in the process of being "smitten." Because we are either immature or head strong, we may ignore blatant signs of incompatibility. It's true we've often heard the comment that opposites attract each other. However, this does not mean that opposites will co-exist or dwell peaceably together in all instances.

I still believe that there is nothing wrong with being smitten. I do believe that you can meet someone and it's as though lightening has struck. I guess it's called "love at first sight." Being smitten is not a bad thing but it does take more than just mushy feelings to make a marriage last. My father used to tell me that love is like an initial spark but can grow into a forest fire. In other words, TRUE LOVE GROWS! In order for that love to grow, the relationship must mature as the people in the relationship mature. For a while we experienced the maturation process but even though smitten, our once blazing forest fire died down to a little brush fire and finally, THE FLAME WENT OUT!

Chapter Four

THE BEGINNING OF THE END

It was a Saturday morning in our home – a day that should have been normal and happy yet I found myself in another heated discussion with my ex-wife. Exactly what was the source of this discussion? Honestly, I don't know. I can't remember anymore. You see, we found ourselves expressing opposing opinions often. It could have been the children, something about the house or likely something else with less significance. Whatever it was, it caused us to enter into a heated debate. I should have become accustomed to this by now because it happened with predictable regularity. In spite of the frequency, I still found that it took something out of me, and I'm sure that it did the same for her. I do know that it took something out of the marriage. I believe that through these discussions, which usually ended in dissidence, we were making constant withdrawals from the marriage and each other without making any deposits. Repeated incidents like this would leave the best marriage first in overdraft and ultimately in bankrupt status.

How could we stop this? That was the million dollar question at the time. I guess if I had the answer we'd probably be together today. We found ourselves arguing even when we promised we wouldn't. It was almost uncontrollable. Maybe we would disagree on something as little as a television show and that disagreement would escalate into something gigantic. After such disagreements I would often reflect and then realize how trivial and mundane they were, but by then it was too late because in the heat of the moment we had uttered angry and damaging words. Unfortunately, you cannot rescind such destructive words.

Well, this day it was especially bad. I had never seen it like this. We never physically fought but some of the words that we allowed to come forth were just as bad. It's called VERBAL ABUSE. We both were pretty good at knowing what to say to attack those sensitive areas of the other's personality. I would hurt her and she would hurt me and from there who knows what we would say. We were pushing all of the buttons and pulling out all of the stops!

I certainly know that words have power – power to build up or power to tear down. I should have known this because I have read it in the Bible time and time again: *Death and life are in the power of the tongue.* Maybe that was the problem. It got to the point that we used words for the purpose of tearing down rather than building up. I have since wondered if we had chosen to use our words to edify or build up rather than to be injurious how different our marriage might have been.

Finally, she could take no more. I guess this particular day I won the argument. Or, did I? In retrospect, I'm not proud of winning because actually I lost. My father used to say that when two people argue for over five minutes neither of them is sure about the validity of their argument and both of them are acting as fools. Well, I guess that day I was the bigger fool. She packed some things and left home.

In the beginning, I was cool. I certainly thought that she wasn't going far. Maybe she would go shopping or ride around until she cooled off and then come home and we would apologize and make up. After all, that was the normal pattern, but this time was different.

The hours went by. I watched the clock as it ticked slowly – six o'clock, seven o'clock then eight o'clock. She wasn't coming home! I'll never forget how I felt when I realized that something was different. She would not be here tonight. Where was she?

By now I became more concerned and then worried. My anger had long since disappeared. My wife, at that time, was out there somewhere and I didn't know where she was or if she was all right. A thousand thoughts went through my mind in a matter of seconds. Maybe she had been in a car accident. Maybe she committed suicide. I had been pretty rough on her. I had allowed some deadly words to come from my mouth. After she left all I could think about is the fact that I couldn't live without her. Oh no! I hated to think about this one: maybe she was with someone else! All of these things terrified me.

After foolishly agonizing over the possibilities and letting go of my pride, I picked up the phone and called her cell phone. It rang and rang but there was no answer. Maybe she had stepped out of the car. I'd try again later.

I called again but as before, no answer. Something must have happened because surely by now she had cooled off. Was she avoiding my calls or could something have really happened? I kept trying and the more I tried the anxiety only increased. In just one day I had gone from rage, to feeling good about winning the argument, to now being nervous because of the uncertainty of her whereabouts. I now felt the tension in my shoulders and back because regardless of our struggles, I still loved her and wanted her to be all right.

After several attempts to reach her, I thought about calling her mother. Surely she would not go to her mother because we had agreed that if we ever got into an argument to the point where one of us left, we would never go to our parents with our problems. We always thought that to go to our parents would make the situation even more difficult. We'd argue and then make up and if we involved our parents they might still have ill feelings towards the "culprit" for hurting their child. So we agreed that in the worst scenario we would take the credit card and go to a hotel and cool off.

I don't know why I didn't remember this pact we had made much earlier. That had to be it! It was almost like something hit me over the head. She was in a hotel, but which one? Was she in our town or some other location? I could have, but I certainly didn't want to call every hotel.

All of a sudden it was like the Lord showed me exactly where she was. There was a certain hotel that we would stay in when we would go home to visit. That's where she had to be. I had stayed there so many times for home visits and preaching engagements until I knew the number by memory. I dialed the number and asked to be connected to her room. And yes, she was registered! The phone rang but there was no answer so I left a message. What a relief! At least I knew that she was all right.

The next morning I got up, fed my children, went to church and preached to my congregation. My heart was hurting. It felt as though my life was falling apart. This was not the way it was supposed to be. The woman I loved and the mother of my children had been driven from our home in anger and frustration. As her husband, I could not deliver the peace required to provide the glue for our relationship. Our parents could not fix it. Neither could the children. I thank God for an overcoming anointing because in His mercy and consideration of His people, His Word went forth mightily that day in spite of delivery through a tormented, wounded, and hurting vessel.

The next day she came home and we discussed the situation. There was little resolution but at least she was back in our home and safe; however, from that point on our marriage suffered. Of course, I am speaking in retrospect. Maybe had I realized how bad things were going I could have tried to stop the bleeding of the emotional wounds inflicted in our relationship. I still did not fully grasp the gravity of the matter.

I'm certainly not saying that this single incident ended the marriage but it certainly revealed that we had more severe problems than I thought at first. It was a turning point. It was the precursor of a waiting tsunami. The big wave was on the way!

What happened?

I don't know what happened. All I know is that I experienced the beginning of the end of the most sacred relationship in my life. In the very beginning, we had a pretty good marriage. We were in love and having fun. I felt that my marriage was as solid as a rock even though there were challenges. I was happy; I was blessed. You may ask how can two people who love each other (no physical violence, no drugs or alcohol abuse, no sexual abuse) enjoy each other for years and end up in divorce court. **We did not realize that a marriage is not a 100-meter dash; instead it's a marathon.** A dash is a race for speed; a marathon is a race for endurance. It is obvious that our marriage was a marriage of speed and not endurance. When you endure you learn to put up with the pain of pressing. It is what the Bible calls LONGSUFFERING; this is the ability to put up with.

Though I have never run a marathon, I do frequently run four miles without stopping. It takes me about forty-five to fifty minutes to run these four miles. Given the time it takes me, you can tell that I'm not running for speed. I get a good little trot and keep going until I reach the finish line. While I'm running I sometimes experience shortness of breath but I keep running. I sometimes feel a pain in my side but I keep running. There have been times when my body felt as if it was about to break but I kept running.

Sometimes I see some guys out on the track who run fast and while I'm running they will pass me only to give out and stop a little later. I have learned to keep my pace and I eventually pass them because I choose to "keep running." A marriage is a marathon. It is something that you keep working on and trying, especially if you believe it's worth it.

Well, what happened? That is the never-ending question. You will discover from reading this book that no one thing happened. There are many things that can affect a marriage. I think that because of this I became caught up with my career. That certainly didn't make the marriage better. Sometimes pastors can become totally involved in saving others and end up losing what we have. Of course, this is not a problem exclusive to pastors. Many professionals become so preoccupied with their careers that other important things are placed on the back burner. This is not just for professionals. Sometimes mothers become so consumed with raising children until they forget husbands. There are many darts that can let the air out of a marriage.

This could be a cause and effect situation. Either I became caught up more in my ministry because of the problems in my marriage or because I was caught up in my ministry the problems in my marriage occurred. I don't know exactly why, but I do know that both happened.

Then there is the element of Satan. Christians and religious folk know who I'm talking about. Satan can be embodied in many people and things, whatever he chooses and whatever we allow. I can testify that Satan is not a fan of marriage. Marriage was instituted by God and anything that God made, Satan continues to unmake. Was it Satan? I'm sure he played his part, but I can't say that it was totally his fault.

I was not aware that our problems were serious; at least serious enough to consider divorce. Honestly, I'm ashamed to say this but I didn't know until the first time she asked for a divorce that it was that bad. That's how out of touch I was. The first time she asked for a divorce was about three years before it actually occurred. Then, we went through times when she would ask for a divorce and then I would ask for a divorce; she would leave the house and the next time I would leave the house. Just a mess! Even then I didn't think that the situation was critical. My God, we were in love! A part of me thought that was just the way marriage was. I thought that she was just expressing dissatisfaction. Even with that I was just like many in the body of Christ who thought that all we needed was prayer. Never did I believe that it would end up in divorce.

Unfortunately, sometimes Christians will use prayer as a substitute for not doing what we should do. Don't get me wrong I really believe in the power of prayer, but I also believe that there are steps we must take as we believe God for answers and assistance. Here I was having problems, praying but still doing the same thing that I had done all along to contribute to the problem.

Again, I don't know exactly what happened! I have shared some of the things that occurred and I could share many more things. Some of these things were not the problem but mere symptoms of the problem. These before mentioned factors are certainly significant but now we are back to that thing called cause and effect. There was obviously a deeper problem that caused these things to occur. We must deal with the root of the issue if we are going to bring resolution. All I know is that our once rock solid marriage grew rocky. It was like a snow ball effect. It was going downhill fast and most of the time I was not aware because I was in my own little world and doing my own little thing. When I became aware of the situation it was out of control. The worst feeling in the world is when you are used to being in control of situations and now all of a sudden you are out of control.

It's sort of like the time that I was on the plane preparing for another flight to some preaching destination. I still remember the feeling I had on this day. I have flown many times and have had many experiences but none like this one. As I walked to the plane from that small airport in Columbus, MS I felt the drizzle on my head. It was nothing significant, just a little precipitation. I boarded the plane, took my seat and fastened my seat belt. We taxied to the runway when all of a sudden a major storm hit. Of course I've never been too comfortable with flying but this time was more uncomfortable than others. Because of the storm, we found ourselves motionless on the runway for hours. For one of the few times in my life I experienced uncomfortable moments where I knew I was definitely not in control. Had I been in the terminal, I could have chosen not to board the plane. Now on the plane, I could not deplane; I couldn't walk to the cock-pit and maneuver the plane. I was forced to just sit there. The situation was out of my control.

All of us have experienced a similar situation in life. Fortunately or unfortunately, there are situations beyond our control. We would love to guide every facet of life but the fact of the matter is that's impossible. There are times when all of our efforts fail and we must give in to the inevitable. One wise person said that patience is a virtue but waiting is a must. There are some things that are out of our control and so the best thing to do is to patiently wait. Regardless of whether I waited patiently or not, I still had to wait. I was experiencing the beginning of the end of my marriage and it was out of my control.

Another incident comes to mind concerning waiting when I was pastor in that small town in Mississippi called Pachuta. In order to get to the church, there was one way in and one way out and I had to cross a train track. Sometimes I would be behind schedule and the train would stop on the track and just remain there. It was then that I learned what I just shared with you: **Patience is a virtue but waiting**

is a must. There was absolutely nothing that I could do. I had to wait! Now the smart thing was to wait patiently. In these instances I needed to just sit back, relax, and read my lesson until the conductor decided to move the train. I'm almost ashamed to tell you that most of the time in the beginning that's not what I did. In spite of my preferences, the matter was out of my control.

By this time, my marriage was out of control. We tried going away together and that was disastrous. We bought a new car and that good feeling was temporary. We went to counseling. Actually, it's funny now when I think about the counselor being so dumbfounded by our situation. I will tell you this, things got so ugly until the counselor advised us to separate! Nothing was working. It was out of my control. As much as we loved them, the kids could not keep us together. Our good status in the community couldn't do it. It was obvious that divorce was inevitable. The worst feeling in the world to me was to not be in control of the outcome of this situation.

A Dream Dies

I had just finished conducting revival in a city and returned home on the next day, which was Saturday. I was sitting outside just relaxing and meditating on the fact that I had to preach several sermons the following day. Suddenly, it crossed my mind that I had no more energy to make my marriage work. It was like an emotional bankruptcy. My account had totally been withdrawn. I called my wife, at that time, to come outside. I talked with her about a sermon that I had preached in one of my Sunday services not long before. I never will forget that it was from the book of Amos. *How can two walk together unless they agree?* That Sunday morning I read from the New Living Translation of the Bible which read: *"How can two walk together unless they agree on the direction?"* My sermon that day was not about marriage but it was about relationships.

She came out, sat down, and we began to talk about our marriage in a way that was more peaceful than we had talked in a long time. It was like the calm after the storm. There was no arguing or negative exchange of words. We talked and it was amazing how that same sermon was on her mind also. For a change, we were on one accord. Unfortunately, we were on one accord concerning divorce. It was a sad day for me. I was losing the person whom I had previously pledged my life and love to. It is kind of like what Job said – *that thing that I feared the most has finally come to pass.* One of the most difficult things to do in life is to let go. I believe that if you really love someone and your relationship with them is not working then love will make you let go because ultimately your desire is to see them happy. Of course letting go is a process. I will address this in another chapter.

I had it all—a beautiful wife, two beautiful kids, a beautiful house, nice cars and a good bank account. And, it's all gone. That dream, that thing that I believed my father and mother instilled in me had now come to an end. So many questions were racing through my mind. Where would I go from here? How could I recover? Would I recover? That was the beginning of the end of a sixteen-year marriage.

Chapter Five

A DEAD MAN PREACHING

O ften in life it is necessary to "die to self" so that we can seek God in His fullest. Ironically, it is in this barren place and seemingly non-productive state that we first learn to trust Him completely. Paul spoke of having to die daily. We can also be so wounded and affected by the turmoil in our lives that we enter a kind of emotional death even though we are alive. I felt the need to die to those things that caused me to neglect my relationship. I felt a second kind of death as I continued to try to live without so many things that meant so much to me.

The last days of my marriage and the following months represent the saddest time of my entire life. I lived and breathed yet it felt as though a portion of me had been buried. Perhaps you remember the seventies tune in which

Dionne Warwick poignantly describes a house which no longer functions as a real home. This song was later recorded by the late Luther Vandross.

I had now experienced estrangement. My household had joined the statistics which identify "broken homes." In reality, I no longer had a home. I had a place to go and sleep at night (a pretty nice apartment); however, it lacked any of the qualities that I would describe as a real home. Even though I traveled a great deal, there was something special about getting off the plane and going home after a ministry engagement, even if that former home had more than its share of misunderstanding and discord. The new dwelling did not afford the opportunity to open the door to my son's and daughter's bedrooms and look in on them as I entered the house from the trip. I could not go into a bedroom, prepare for bed, and fall asleep beside the woman I loved. It was over. The new place was empty, void of my children's laughter, void of the nuisance of toys and books on the floor and completely lacking the qualities which would have made it a real home. It was just a place to sleep.

Later, my darling daughter, then 13 years old, mentioned that I appeared to be sad all of the time. She was right. I felt lonely, displaced, forsaken, and frustrated. I had no home. I had square footage, nice carpet, and a lease! At that point the most palatial dwelling on earth could not replace what I had lost.

Clinton, Jr., my beloved son and namesake, then 8 years old, wondered if perhaps he had done something so terrible that it had caused me and his mother to decide that we would no longer live together. This still brings sadness to my heart because I realized the enemy was capable of invading the mind of a child and convincing him that he was a major villain in the breakup of a marriage. Nothing could have been further from the truth! After all, true to his job description, *the enemy is an accuser of the brethren.* He's so ruthless and merciless that he has no problem planting this same condemnation in the tender heart of an innocent and loving child.

I love both of my children so much. I regret any agony that they internalized.

The church congregation displayed genuine concern for me as well as for my former wife, who had now left the congregation. Some members who were really close enough to discern the depth of my pain, prayed for me constantly. I could not allow the full membership to know that their pastor felt as though he was about to lose his mind. Dependent upon their maturity in their walk with the Lord, many depended upon me to help to sustain their faith.

My parents, siblings and one brother especially, stayed close by my side. The board of deacons was especially supportive. They knew my heart and displayed special male sensitivity for my obvious discomfort in being detached from my family. Many times they expressed willingness to help to care for them during the time I was on the road. I knew that in times of emergency that I could count on them to go to my home and assist my family. They knew how much I cared. My brother and I would go out and have dinner together, especially after church on Sunday. I appreciated him being there. Otherwise, I would have just gone home and cried.

Ironically, during this time I often ministered under an unusual and powerful anointing to the congregation and larger community in which the church was located. I could literally feel burdens lifted and the souls of others being set free; but I, the pastor, could hardly keep from falling apart after being used as a vessel to bless so many. I actually prayed for the marriages of others and saw healing take place. Sometimes I wanted to ask God again, "Did you call the wrong man?" "Am I being punished?" "What's going on?" "What can I do to remove this bitter cup?"

I was a dead man preaching! It always amazed me as to how God continued to use me in such a powerful and pre-vailing way in spite of the fact that I was emotionally frail and finite. I guess this is what the Apostle Paul discovered about God in the midst of some of his most challenging times. He wrote to the Corinthian church concerning a thorn that he dealt with constantly. He wanted God to remove this aggravation. After God informed him that He would not remove it but would give him grace to deal with it, Paul then discovered something about himself and said, *"When I am weak, then am I strong."*

It is so amazing how strong I remained in my preaching even when many times I would be in agony right before walking into the pulpit. After preaching I would feel that same emptiness. Thank God that the gift of ministry didn't suffer. Painfully, I still recall that worthless feeling that would engulf me as I changed my clothes, wet from perspiration, in the pastor's office. I would have just preached with great intensity about God's goodness and how He could turn things around in your life; but, the reality was that things were not turning around in my life; or so I thought.

There are many episodes of personal emptiness that I could share in this book but I will only share a few. The thing which blesses me most is that God did not lift His precious anointing.

I was conducting a revival at a friend's church and the power of God used me as a vessel to bless the people in such a way until I almost felt an out-of-body experience. During that time, I was preaching through my pain and was obviously able to connect with a hurting congregation because of my own condition. I discovered that there is a better connection when we are able to communicate our own experiences. I had experienced hurt and loss but God sustained me and enabled me to effectively bless others who were in the midst of a similar circumstance.

Another instance occurred at my beloved Southside Baptist Church. It was Sunday morning. I went to church about an hour early to meditate. It started out as one of my depressed days. While I was in my office it seemed as if all of the pain of my problems crashed down upon me like a ton of bricks. I started crying and praying. I remember that this was shortly before the divorce was final. Because of this awful feeling, I just didn't want to preach. I don't know, maybe it was just too painful or I could have been upset with God. You see, I felt forsaken by God. I remember telling Him, Lord, I know that I'm not perfect and I did many things that I'm not proud of, but I also did many things for your glory. Why would you allow this to happen to me? It was at that point that I could see how others felt when they loved God, paid their tithes, went to church and treated others right; but tragic things occurred anyhow.

I'm glad that the forsaken feeling did not remain long. Because of my study of God's Word and the longevity of my walk, I knew that sometimes things will happen regardless of your foundation in the faith. Even though the ill feelings were sometimes prevalent and I occasionally blamed God, I discovered that I was definitely under-equipped to box with him. On this particular Sunday, whatever the emotional state, I concluded that I was not preaching.

I wondered how could I get up and preach to the people when I didn't even want to look at them. You must understand that at this time I was dealing not only with hurt but embarrassment as well. It was most embarrassing to have preached so many sermons concerning marriage only to lose yours. I remember conducting a seminar for one of our local churches on "How to Connect with Your Spouse" and now I had no spouse. My name circulated in the rumor mill. I was very humiliated and decided I would not preach on this day.

I called my first assistant's office and asked him to come to my office. When he arrived, I informed him that I was not preaching today and he would have to minister. I told him to get one of his sermons and do his best because I was going back home to get in bed. As usual the church was filling up. I didn't even care that this was a very awkward and difficult position to put a preacher in. All pastors and preachers know that when a congregation is expecting to hear their pastor it is difficult for another to fill his shoes.

Hundreds of people were filling the sanctuary to hear me preach, and I was sending this guy out like a sheep to the slaughter. I didn't care; I was a dead man! I could tell that he was nervous as well as worried about me. When he left my office, he went and got one of the deacons of the church who always had my ear and trust. This man was a prayer warrior. They knocked on my door as I was packing to leave and asked if they could pray with me. I answered in the affirmative and proceeded to bow my head. After praying, they left and I resumed packing.

All of a sudden, I felt God's presence all over me like never before. I felt His reassurance and confirmation informing me of the fact that He had not left me or forsaken me, and He never would. I cried and shouted at the same time in my office all by myself. I stayed back there and had my own private time with God. I actually feel His presence right now as I recall this tremendous reassurance.

Right before time to preach, I entered the sanctuary. I could see relief on the faces of the congregation and especially the slated substitute preacher. I walked over to him and said, "I GOT IT!" My original message for that day was dismissed. Instead, the Lord led me to preach from Isaiah chapter 40:

He gives power to the faint and to them that have no might He increases strength. Even the youth shall faint and be weary and the young men shall utterly fall. But they that wait upon the Lord shall renew their strength. They shall run and not be weary; they shall walk and not faint.

My God, what a day! The house went up in "heavenly smoke" and the people were blessed like never before. They were blessed from a dead man preaching. I learned something that day that I shall never forget. It's not me but the Christ who lives in me. Without Him, I am nothing. I also learned that God can use me just as I am – broken, hurt, and confused.

Paul explained it like this, *"God has placed this treasure in earthen vessels."* In full agreement, the late Dr. William Augustus Jones says that God has put **"treasure in trash."** I was trash BUT God was still using me to bless so many people.

I PRAISE God for carrying me through.

I HONOR Him for sustaining me in a deep and horrible pit.

I TRUST Him as a deliverer when I thought I couldn't make it.

I ADORE Him for allowing His Spirit and Anointing to remain with me.

I BLESS Him for His Word, which heals and forgives.

A DEAD MAN STILL TRYING

Just before the divorce was final I was ministering in a city in Florida. I was so distraught with the pending action that I contemplated calling my estranged wife to see if some kind of reconciliation was possible. I, like many men, had my fair share of egotism; however, I put it all aside and decided to do just that. I wanted to verbalize my willingness to forget everything, start all over again and rebuild what we had once shared together. I had just left a ministry engagement where the host pastor and his wife almost ended their marriage. Somehow they worked it out. After sharing my situation with him that pastor encouraged me to try to do the same. I promised him I would try once again.

I was willing to court her, bedazzle and stop just short of turning water into wine. (You already know that working miracles is a Jesus thing. He has wisely not entrusted water conversion into wine to me). I am just trying to illustrate how desperate I was at that point. Sometimes we brag about the things we would never do—the things we would not stoop to—the things we wouldn't take. I ate many of those words during this time. Believe me, all egotism went out the window as I once again genuinely professed deep love for the woman who won my heart, took my name, and gave me children. This was a long, honest, and passionate plea for her to reconsider.

I was a dead man and felt that the only way I could experience resurrection was to get my family back. I felt that I had lost it all when I lost her. She was my reason for doing what I did. I know that this is not the right thing, but sometimes we can develop an improper perspective of priorities. Just like most husbands and fathers, I did most of what I did because of my desire to provide for my family. Now that she was out of my life, I felt like my drive was gone. What was the catchy phrase in the movie about Stella? **I lost my groove!** I needed my groove back, and it happened to be this woman whom I had pledged my love to.

After I had finished my preaching assignment, I was then taken to the airport. I made it to the airport and waited for my flight to begin boarding. I called her. I expressed all my feelings to her. I apologized for those things that I did to contribute to the breakup of the marriage. I shared with her how empty I was without her and how I felt God wanted us to remain in holy matrimony; but, most importantly, I wanted her back.

I paused after about a 15-minute monologue to wait for her response. Well, the response was not what I wanted to hear. I will not go into what she said, but I felt like I had been pierced again. It was not that she was rude; for she was very soft spoken, understanding, and tactful. I really felt that she did everything in her power to spare my feelings; yet, her words fell short of what I wanted to hear.

Her mind was made up. She had found happiness, fulfillment and relief without me! I guess the pressure over the years had just been too great. Again, I can't blame her. I share responsibility for not being a better husband in the manner SHE needed.

As painful as the whole matter might have been, I discovered that for the sake of survival, it was necessary to bury myself even more in the work of developing the local ministry and efforts in national evangelism for the Kingdom until God gave further direction. So, I forged ahead with Jesus as a much-needed intercessor.

I confess. I am much more human than Divine. Consequently, I will not pretend that I was not lonely. I still felt tremendous hurt. I still cried; but somehow, I made it. However, I learned some valuable lessons during this wilderness experience. Included among these lessons were compassion, humility, longsuffering, selflessness (not selfishness), and the merit of praise and adoration even in tough times. God was at work in me and had gone before me to prepare a way of escape. I was on the potter's wheel and was being expertly handled by the Master for presentation as a better vessel. His gentle clay-stained hand dried my tears and the pressure of His foot on the pedal of the wheel kept me in forward and perpetual motion though sometimes it hurt.

Never forget that God is with you through the deepest and most tragic of circumstances. His method and timing may not be aligned with our desires and urgent schedules, but I am a living witness that ultimately, His way works. EVERYTIME! Just trust Him!

If your **HEART** is **RIGHT** and your **MOTIVES** are **GODLY**, and **IF** you are **COMMITTED** to **SERVE** Him then He obligates Himself to **BRING YOU THROUGH!** Remember that Clinton McFarland told you so when you reach the other side of torrential waters. I can speak with such confidence because in His word I found confirmation: *When you pass through the waters, I will be with you; and when you pass through the rivers, they will not sweep over you. When you walk through the fire, you will not be burned; the flames will not set you ablaze.*

More than ever in my entire life, I ascertained more about God during this trying time. One of the things that I learned is to not give up and throw in the towel. By virtue of the fact that I had breath in my body, God was still good. I then looked at my life and started counting my blessings. **I looked not at what I had lost but what I had left.** Ultimately, I learned, not from academic research, but from the school of hard knocks that God loves even an emotionally dead man. I could still preach this priceless and precious Gospel.

The divorce became final and I kept on LIVING and PREACHING!

Chapter Six

AN EMOTIONAL ROLLER COASTER

Well it's over. I'm now divorced. Wow! I can't begin to explain to those of you who have not experienced the trauma of divorce how it feels. I must say that there was no shortage of emotional challenges. It seemed like a different set of emotions paid me a visit every day. The real challenge was that I never knew which one would show up on any given day. One day I was mad and the next day hurt, then I became lonely. The next day I felt bitter, and the next day I was subjected to jealousy. I really have great difficulty adequately explaining how I felt. My heart and feelings were going through the same kind of uncertainty as one feels on that gigantic ride at the amusement park.

In my younger years, I was intrigued by amusement parks. I was particularly drawn to the roller coasters. I remember traveling to a park in Ohio where there was a ride called "The Gemini." It was a massive roller coaster known at that time as one of the largest and most exciting in the world. I approached it and stood in a line for over an hour just to get a two minute and twenty second ride. After fastening into my seat, I buckled up for the ride. It took me up about one hundred and twenty-five feet almost straight up in the air. Uh-uh! I became really nervous because I knew that when you go that high the only way back to your starting point is—DOWN!

Did it take me down? You bet it did! It took me down with accelerated and horrific speed, but one of the exciting things about the roller coaster was its unpredictable pattern. I never knew what was coming next. It took me up, down, round and around and even upside-down. I guess now you can see why I entitled this part of my book AN EMOTIONAL ROLLER COASTER.

I found great similarities in riding a roller coaster and going through a divorce. One of the real issues for me was that I was not prepared. The mood swings came unexpectedly. I did not see them coming. In fact, I don't think that anyone can fully prepare for the re-adjustment period after the finalization of divorce proceedings.

I remember going to the county courthouse to meet my attorney so that we could file the final decree. It was a rainy cold November night. I was crying and very sad because of how traumatic this whole process had been. All I could think about was that it was finally over. Sixteen years of marriage went down the drain. I felt like such a failure. I must admit that just recounting this part of my life is still difficult. Even though it has been several years, it is almost like reliving that uneasy night all over again.

A thousand thoughts flashed in and out of my mind. I thought about our wedding day at her mother's house. We didn't have a large church wedding; just a small gathering with a few friends and family members. I thought about the good times and the bad. Even though there were some bad days, I must admit that there were many more good days. This contributed greatly to my sadness, and mentally processing all of this produced great anxiety.

I got out of my car and walked through security into the courthouse. After entering the clerk's office I caught a view of my attorney chatting with some of the office personnel. Everyone greeted me.

"Hello, Reverend McFarland."

I said hello and tried to be as nonchalant as possible in an effort to camouflage my countenance. I proceeded to a designated area and received a pen to affix my signature to a document that would wipe it all away—the wedding, the years together, and my life as I had known it.

"Mr. McFarland, would you sign here, here, and here?"

I signed the document that would forever change my life. At that point, I was no longer married. My attorney smiled and said, "I know you should be relieved."

"Yes," I said, and for just a moment or two, I did feel a kind of RELIEF.

Why was I relieved? Was it because of the months of negotiation that transpired between our attorneys? Was it because I was now FREE? Was it because at least now I didn't have to speculate as to what my financial obligations would be? Was it because of the strain of the last years of marriage? I didn't know. In fact, I still don't know why I was relieved, but this sense of relief didn't last!

The roller coaster was now in motion. It started like other roller coasters – really nice and pleasant. It took me up, up, and up. I remember thinking, "Hey, this is not so bad. I'm young, black, and gifted. I have my nice little apartment and a great job. This is not so bad. Even though I was not in favor of a divorce, I felt okay.

That's how a roller coaster starts. Unfortunately, that feeling was short lived. From day to day I could never predict my feelings.

I went from feeling relieved to feeling REJECTED. How could this end like this? I know that I wasn't the best husband but I certainly wasn't the worst. I knew guys who had been far worse than I had been but their wives stuck it out. I was a good provider, protector, and parent. I gave my love and my life to her but she didn't want me anymore. I was an unwilling passenger on this particular ride.

Rejection is an awful emotion. It is even worse when you experience rejection by someone whom you particularly desire. This was a great hurdle for the person who wanted to stay in the marriage. It was a great leap. You love this person and though you are no longer in the relationship, you still desire their affection and affirmation.

I experienced this. It certainly didn't do much for my self-esteem.

I began to wonder if something was wrong with me. Rejection played an emotional game with my mind. Those of us who have experienced rejection have to be very careful because it can have a great affect on the next relationship. Sometimes it plants a thought in the back of your mind that maybe the next person will eventually reject you as well. It makes it hard to totally love again. You tend to keep up your guard and inevitably place barriers in the relationship. If the next relationship is going to be successful, it is important that you consciously not allow this to happen.

Not long after, my emotional roller coaster ride took a turn from rejection to RESENTMENT. What an awful turn! I was now bitter. I felt that I had wasted all those years with this woman and now look at my life. I was a hard working man who never required my wife to work outside of the home. I knew that she dreamed of being a homemaker and a full-time mother. I made it happen, and for what?

The resentment continued to build and I thought about all of the jobs that I had worked just to be a good provider. I reflected upon the sacrifices that I had to make. I'm certainly not saying that she did not make any sacrifices but at that time I was not thinking about that. All I could think about was I was trying to build a future; so I worked hard. I was the breadwinner! (I was maybe a little selfish in my thinking. I don't know.)

According to the divorce decree, I was still the breadwinner. Yes, I agreed to the terms of the divorce but felt that to some degree it was not fair. I always felt that it was right that I would continue to financially provide for a certain period of time because of the fact that she could not survive otherwise; but at times I resented it like crazy. Whether you agree with me or not, the fact that it bothered me is not up for debate; that's just how I felt. I resented a lot of things, but you must remember that I was on this emotionally-charged ride.

I went to bed one night bitter and awoke the next morning BROKEN. Oh my God, here is another turn. I'm broken about the fact that it is really over. Divorced! ME? Not in my wildest dreams. All of my dreams of growing old and being able to say like others, "We have been married for fifty years," crumbled and that possibility was now slim. I'm broken about the fact that I can't see my children before they go to bed at night. I can't kiss them prior to them going to school.

And then there is more brokenness. I'm overwhelmed and broken with the settling reality that we are not together.

There is just something about divorce that will just break you down! I've never considered myself a cry-baby but I must admit that this regularly brought tears to my eyes. I was an emotionally broken mess. I always considered myself to be a strong man, but this situation crushed my past strength. I was BROKEN! I experienced these emotions for many days.

Now, it's a new day! The sun is shining and the birds are singing. I feel pretty good today after crying all night. My roller coaster has hit a good spot. Along the way there have been some fairly good days too. This seems to be one. I'm experiencing another incline. Up, up, up and away!

It sure does look beautiful from here. Today, I have conquered an emotional incline from broken to BLISS. I am blissful that there are no more arguments. There is no more compromise. Whatever decision I make I don't have to consult with anyone. I'm my OWN man. I'm catching the plane to go and preach in some fabulous city with no one to say, "You're gone too much!" Oh what joy! Maybe it's all over – I mean the emotional rollercoaster ride from this point on. Surely, it will be smooth sailing.

I have now made it to the airport, and I'm ready to catch my flight. I'm feeling so much joy thinking that the worst is over, but that was short lived. My rollercoaster, after taking a short incline, has now hit a severe dip from joy to JEALOUSY!

While walking through the airport, I run into a couple holding hands. They recognize me.

"Hello, Pastor McFarland. Where are you headed to preach tonight?"

"Richmond, Virginia." I responded and then asked them, "Where are you two lovebirds going today?"

"We are headed to the Bahamas for a little romantic getaway."

DIP! DIP! DIP! Jealousy overtook me. It's not that I was jealous of them and their relationship, but I thought about why that could not be me. Why am I alone and it seems as if everybody has somebody? I'm sorry that was just the emotional state that I was in.

I'm sure that I could have found companionship but that's just a temporary fix if it's not with the one you love. I know that Luther Vandross sang **that if you can't be with the one you love then love the one you are with**; but that's just a song. Songs sound good, they rhyme and tickle the ear, but the message conveyed doesn't always work in real life.

If she didn't want to be with me then there must have been someone else. Who was he? You do know that is just a natural reaction whenever you are overcome with jealousy. Actually, all kinds of thoughts went through my mind. I had to try to deal with this one quickly because jealousy will make you do some things that you will later regret. I would be ashamed to mention some of my deliberations.

I was miserable this entire trip thinking about the fact that she was probably with someone else. My imagination did not help because it played a real game with me. What made it even worse was that I engaged in a conversation with someone who felt like I felt and reassured me that she probably was with someone else. Of course, I don't think that was the case immediately, but if it's in your mind it becomes a reality to you.

These are only a few examples of the emotions that I felt after the dissolution of the marriage. It would take another fifty pages to adequately describe this rollercoaster ride. I must admit, unlike the quick ride at amusement parks, this particular ride takes years to end. Why is this so?

Divorce represents a form of death. Even though death is the end of life, I feel that sometimes divorce is even worse.

I remember when one of my closest friends was stricken with a fatal disease. He dealt with this infirmity for many years. I remember the day that his wife called to tell me of his turn for the worst. She and his two sons met me upon my arrival at the hospital. What could I say? After all, this guy was like a brother to me and his wife, like a sister.

I walked into the room to visit him and tried to communicate with him. He could not talk but I believe that he could understand me. I said something to him that seemed to ease all of his worries. Shortly thereafter, the doctor came in and I left the room to go and comfort his family.

Later the doctor came to tell us that all of his organs had ceased to function. He had died!

I will never forget a lump in my throat and the speechlessness that I experienced like never before. What an awful feeling. I still miss him. But as awful as this was, enduring a divorce was an even worse feeling. Of course, I'm speaking for me only, but I have talked with people who feel the same.

Why is this so? I believe that when one dies we inevitably have to accept the things that we cannot change. Death represents carnal finality. Death means that it's physically over. We cry and go through the grieving process, but it's over. Divorce, like death, is the severing of a relationship but it does not really represent finality immediately.

I held out for hope but enveloped in that hope was hurt. It was like the amputation of a leg. You will live without the leg but not without the painful adjustments. Sometimes it is even essential for the leg to be amputated because of the poison that has overtaken it. That poison can spread throughout the body and ultimately destroy it. Amputation is sometimes necessary but always painful.

Those of you who have been through divorce know what I'm talking about, particularly when you were married for many years. Hopefully, those of you who have not experienced divorce can understand why I said that for me divorce was more difficult than death.

The good news is that you can make it if you allow this ride to run its inescapable course. Yes, some things are inescapable. We are human beings and emotional people. When there are situations and circumstances that trigger certain emotions, we must understand that some of this is natural. Jesus Christ was an emotional man. He went into the temple and saw that the worship was out of order. He then allowed his emotions to move him to do something about the situation.

In another instance, He went to visit some friends in a little town call Bethany. Mary and Martha had lost their brother Lazarus. The Bible states that when Jesus went to the grave; HE WEPT. I'm not going to devote a great deal of discussion to the reason that he wept; but the fact is that he did. He experienced emotions. Perhaps the weeping represented His humanness and His divine mission to bring healing not just to Himself, but also for many, including YOU and ME!

The good news is – there is healing. God can heal us from whatever ails us.

I believe that some emotions must run their course in order for the healing to begin in your life. Might I suggest that you deal with this emotional roller coaster with a prayerful spirit? I suggest that you take it to the Lord in prayer.

One of the most inspiring songs that I sing to myself in the midst of trying times is "What a Friend We Have in Jesus."

What a friend we have in Jesus

All our sins and grief to bear

What a privilege it is to carry

Everything to God in prayer

Oh what peace we often forfeit

Oh what needless pain we bear

All because we do not carry

Everything to God in prayer

I would suggest that you try singing this hymn when you are going through a trial. I promise it will make your roller coaster ride much better so that the healing can begin.

For me healing did begin, but not without additional challenges. I wish that I could tell you that the hurt and drama ended there but it didn't. Are you familiar with earthquakes? If you are, then you know that just as it is with any earthquake, there are aftershocks!

Chapter Seven

A SERIES OF AFTER-SHOCKS

The process of going through divorce proceedings is progressive. First, there is the pain of acceptance or denial of failure; then there is the anxiety of physical and emotional separation. Later however, just as with a powerful earthquake, a wave of aftershocks begin to rock the lives of all involved. Sometimes these waves are as troubling as the initial onslaught.

The 2010 major earthquake that so devastated the little country of Haiti remains fresh in my memory. I can still visualize the vivid pictures of the rubbish that was once buildings. It's as though the images are permanently imprinted in my mind. Thousands of people died and many more were displaced as a result of this catastrophic and cataclysmic occurrence.

As I watched many hours of news coverage to try and get a better understanding of just how devastating this disaster was, an aftershock hit. I saw people running and dispersing, trying to get out of harm's way. It was reported by the newscaster that the aftershocks kept occurring and that these post tremors were actually worse, in some cases, than the earthquake itself.

The individual who has experienced a divorce faces emotional consequences or episodes similar to an earthquake, but the divorce is not the end of the disaster. The unfortunate aftershocks are just as damaging as the earthquake itself. Little did I know this so I was not prepared for many of the things that occurred later. I realized that I seemed to have survived the big one, but what about these aftershocks? Why did my world continue to reel and rock?

When Children are involved

Divorce is not just an issue for the couple; it is just as much an issue for the children. Yes, children are flexible but not immune to the ill effects connected with the breakup of their parents. You would be surprised at how many parents believe that children are not adversely affected by divorce.

I have heard parents say, "They will be all right." The fact is they possibly will be all right but not without proper attention given to their emotions. We have to be careful because kids are very good at internalizing things, but inevitably what they internalize will come out and most of the time these feelings will emerge in a negative way. You have seen it happen time and time again. Sometimes the outcome of their internalization of the problem is manifested in a drug or alcohol addiction, emotional trauma, or worse. Many children of divorced parents enter into sexual relationships at an earlier age. I believe that in some way, they are trying to fill that void.

I can't even begin to describe the pain that this divorce put our children through. I can't tell you because I don't even know the totality of it all, but I do know the part that I observed as a loving parent. I am aware of the questions that were asked. Remember, I shared with you the time that my son asked me if it was something that he did that made me leave home. This was obviously something that he had pondered in his little mind. I also remember the concern of my daughter when she observed my demeanor. I guess my countenance was one of sadness. I tried to camouflage it, but with little success. This was an emotional aftershock that my beloved children dealt with. The real problem is you don't know the magnitude of it immediately. We may never know! I do know that they cherished having a mother and father and a happy home then one day, it all vanished.

Not only were there emotional after-shocks that occurred on the part of our children but also on both of us as parents. I'm sure that my ex-wife experienced some residual effects because regardless of the situation, these feelings are inevitable. Since I can't speak for her situation, I will just address the matter from my perspective.

Can you imagine feeling as if you have lost everything? Once upon a time, you felt as if you had it all. You had the good job, the house, the wife, the children and the dog. Life was at its apex. You were on top of the world. One day you have it and the next, you have lost it all. Well, it didn't happen exactly like that but it seemed that way. I mean I did not lose it all over night. It took some time, but the pain of it all was certainly prevalent after I realized how much I had worked for and how rapidly it disintegrated.

I'm sure that any concerned and caring parent can attest to what I am about to share. The worst part of all of this divorce stuff was the sense of losing my children. They are my pride and joy. Actually I didn't lose them but it seemed like I did. Our relationship was certainly not the same. When I lived in the house with them I remember tucking them in at night. Some nights they would come and get in the bed with me and I would have to make them go to their own beds. There are so many things that I missed that I took for granted when we all lived under the same roof.

When I was a younger man I used to say that I wanted at least ten children, but of course, that changed when I started to be responsible for two. I share this now to illustrate how deeply I felt about the gift of having children. After all, I grew up with seven siblings.

I can remember my childhood in the fondest way. It was probably the best time of my life. Growing up with my four sisters and three brothers meant there was never a dull moment. We did not have many toys or games, but we found creative ways of amusing ourselves. We would have races and tell jokes. We would play cards or kick ball. What a wonderful time in my life.

We were blessed to enjoy a life of stability. Though we were not rich we always had what we needed to survive. My parents were hard working people, and were dedicated to the institution of family. They realized that God instituted the family so they took the vows for better or worst seriously. Not that they were perfect; far from it, but they did what was necessary to make it work. They were dedicated to their children and equally committed to raising us properly.

Our home was happy and full of excitement. Both of our parents were there for us in a meaningful way. My mother smothered us with love and my daddy, in addition to being a great provider, laid down the law.

I believe that children should live a life of simplicity, security, and safety. This is the kind of life we lived. We did not have to worry about the vicissitudes of life. Whatever occurred we trusted that our parents could take care of it, especially my dad. Oh my dad! I thought he was a superman. Well I guess he was because he seemed to be able to handle anything. All we had to do was take it to Dad and he could work it out. I am sure that there were so many frustrating days in his life because of his inability to work everything out on a human level; however, we did not know it. For this reason, we felt safe and secure with nothing but fun things to care about. We were very close to our Dad and he was very close to us. I share this with you because I want to convey how I feel about children.

Consequently, I am especially close to the two precious children that I fathered. I had no plans to leave them. Instead, I lamented at the thought that one day, years down the road, they would leave me. I never will forget the birth of Dwanna, my daughter, my princess, and firstborn. Some months earlier I had gone to my ex-wife and shared that I thought that we needed a child. I asked how she felt. She agreed and Dwanna was conceived almost immediately.

I waited anxiously in a waiting room as she went into labor. There were some complications and I was not allowed to be in the room with her. After what seemed to be an eternity, I was allowed to see our prematurely born little girl. She was so tiny – just over four pounds. I could literally hold her in the palm of my hand. Like many fathers, afraid that my hands would not be gentle enough, I was afraid to hold her that first time but I had to! I remember reflecting on how our coming together had actually created something so beautiful, so innocent, and so dependent. I carefully lifted this little bundle of joy to my chest and held her. I gently gave her that first kiss that every little girl deserves from her father. I thanked God for the miracle of this little life.

A few years later Clinton, Jr. blessed our household. As much as I loved the women in our home, I was so glad to have this little man to help me bring "balance" into the household. He too, was a bundle of joy. He grew quickly to be a lot like me—fun loving, meeting no strangers, and having lots to say. We rivaled each other in healthy male competition and video game marathons. From the beginning, I often pulled him aside in an effort to teach him how to be a man.

My children brought tremendous joy to my life, but through divorce, that perfect family scenario was altered somewhat yet, my love remained intact. What an aftershock! Every good parent wants to enjoy raising their children and to see them grow up healthy and whole. Divorce has the potential to negatively affect this desired wholeness even if it is only temporary. I am yet doing all that I have the power to do to make sure that I minimize the effects of these aftershocks in their lives; but some things might be inevitable. So it is my prayer that what I'm unable to do, God will do!

I would like to think that I am a lot like my dad; particularly in my approach to dealing with family. As a father, I still try to give my children what my dad gave to me and more. I wanted them to feel secure and safe, and to never have to concern themselves with the complications of life until it was time. I have seen too many children forced to forfeit childhood because of the irresponsibility of the parents. I have seen children raising their little brother or sister, not because of unforeseen circumstances or a catastrophic event, but because of negligence. This is not what I wanted for my children. It is for this reason that I was against divorce. I still felt that to keep the marriage together was the will of God. Since it was God's will; I operated with the faith that He would give us the strength to make it happen if we did not give up or succumb to the pressure to quit. I had counseled many divorcees and was very much aware of the affects of divorce, particularly on the children. I now reviewed the words of my own counsel and weighed the unfortunate consequences of ending a marriage.

Because my parents had eight children, I watched my father at one time work five different odd jobs because of his responsibility to his family. Since being an adult, I have often thought about how he could have done as many men –walk off into the sunset never to be seen again and leave the struggle to Mom. Now deceased, I must acknowledge he "stuck with it." Even through the toughest times, he was a father and a real man of God. I am thankful he remained married to my mother until his death. They were together for over forty-six years. I guess I felt that if I went through a divorce, I would be walking out on my family. I have since understood that one does not have to neglect his responsibility simply because he no longer lives in the house. Just for the record, I make sure that I take care of my responsibilities as a father in every way. I feel that regardless of what happened to their mother and me, there was no reason for sacrifice on the children's part.

What about the money…..

This leads me to the next aftershock that rocked my world – MONEY! I do not express this with the least complaint, but this certainly proved to be an after-shock. In the beginning, this was a major adjustment. There is no need to disclose the specific financial terms of the divorce but believe me it was significant. Many men understand the difficulty of providing for one household, but imagine two – two electrical power bills, two water bills, two house payments, and the list goes on.

During the marriage, I was the sole provider financially; and after the marriage, I was required to continue the same standard of living that my ex-wife and children were accustomed to. I felt that this was right then and feel the same now. I was required to pay alimony and child support. The law in the state of Mississippi requires this if you are married over ten years and one spouse either does not work outside of the home or makes a considerably lower income than the other. The term of the alimony is up to the judge and based on the length of the marriage and age of the dependant spouse. Thankfully, we chose not to let a judge decide these financial terms. We discussed and debated the amount and eventually came to a mutual agreement with the aid of our attorneys. To this day, I have not gone before a judge on this matter. Our lawyers took the agreement before the judge and the judge agreed and signed it into effect.

I believe that to care for your loved ones is not only required by law but by God for those of us who adhere to the Bible. I was responsible to provide that same financial security that I did when I was in the home. To this day, if for any reason I felt that my children were in any danger or their security was threatened, I would not hesitate to help them. I am financially responsible and make sure that funds are in place in full amount and on time, as promised. I cannot call myself a pastor or a Christian and operate as a deadbeat dad. I did not need a judge to make me fulfill my financial obligations. I was both considerate and generous. Without coercion or outside intervention, I consciously decided to continue to provide a comfortable standard of living. Based on set formulas in domestic settlement issues, a judge probably would have ordered far less.

In spite of my godly duty to my family, I will admit that it was not easy. There were times when I wanted to act out of anger and fight the divorce and the money. It was never a time that I was not willing to compensate my ex-wife and children but to the degree that I did, I experienced apprehension. All kinds of thoughts went through my mind concerning the fact that I was taking care of a woman and I had relinquished the benefit of a relationship or any reciprocation from her. When we were married she washed my clothes, cleaned our house, and did other things that a homemaker would do; but now it had all changed. I had incurred additional expenses and I was spending money to wash my own clothes and clean my own place. I did not think this was totally fair.

I thank God for the advice of a prominent pastor whom I was preaching for at the time who had gone through a similar situation by way of divorce. He gave me the advice that I would give to all men and women who, for whatever reason, fall into this predicament. He advised me first of all not to fight this in court even if you know that you could win. He said, "If you are a man of God then give her whatever she wants and if you do this, I promise that God will not let you suffer."

Thank you, Pastor because you certainly are a prophet. God has so tremendously blessed me, and I believe that it was as a result of my willingness to go the extra mile.

In summary, for a brief period of transition, the dissolution of the marriage rocked my financial world. It represented an aftershock of major proportion. It was only by the grace of God that I was able to make necessary sacrifices, recover, and financially regroup.

Back to the Children...

I now reside in another state. I have accepted the position of Senior Pastor of a church in Atlanta, GA. I have been out of my children's home for some time and it is like a special adventure in culture shock. Much of the earlier pain came back to torment me. I never felt emptier in my life than I did when I was no longer able to see them in their regular routine. I still miss seeing them go to school and coming home. I miss being able to walk to their rooms and check on them. I miss play station sessions with my son and walks to the community store. I must repeat that many of these things that I miss; initially, I took for granted. They became even more precious after

I moved away. There were some things that often I was too tired to do that I would find the strength to do now. I would make an adjustment in scheduling to salvage these precious moments. It is also amazing how, ironically, you even miss some of the most annoying aspects of living in a household. I will not go into these. They don't matter now.

It was not like I was at home a lot because my career kept me away quite a bit. As a result, many of these things I missed regularly but I knew that when I got home they would be there, but these are not the only aftershocks.

When Decisions are made...

Another aftershock was not being involved in the decision making process. Because I was no longer there, many of the decisions made concerning the children were made without my input. I was not the custodial parent. Of course, I am not saying that this is necessarily wrong because it is difficult for two to decide if both are in the home but much more difficult if the parents are living apart—especially if one travels extensively. I accept this now but I have not always understood why this basic responsibility ceased to be mine. I now view this in retrospect. In the beginning, I was inwardly furious. I was furious that I had to get permission to get my own children. Man, that's an after-shock! I was furious that my kids were going places and doing things of which I did not approve. I was furious because it was as though I no longer had a voice in the most important thing in my life. I was most furious that my home was torn apart and my relationship had not weathered the storm like my Mom and Dad's. Somehow, I dealt with it and made it through.

It's a good thing that I got over it before I found out that my teenage daughter was receiving the company of a young man without my consent. I think that I took it like a champ. All things considered, I must add that I think it was a pretty good decision. As I recollect, it was not that she was not at the proper age but I resented the fact that I was not involved. I was deprived of the being able to drill her and question her even when I knew I was going to say yes. You see, parents like that kind of stuff. Oh, but when I found out I did have a heart-to-heart talk with the young fellow. I really enjoyed that! I remember how nervous I made him. Man that was a good day! A good father wants to protect his daughter and secure her environment.

He wants to warn others that she indeed has a covering or someone to protect her.

Even though I learned how to deal with the fact that most decisions were made without me, it was still a rude awakening and extremely painful emotionally.

It was necessary to ask God for grace to continue even if I had failed to duplicate the wonderful model of a home like my father had done. I prayed for a double dose of mercy to get me through this transition and accept the set of circumstances, which dictated new guidelines and restrictions in parenthood. The hymnist penned my heart's sentiment so eloquently in the hymn "Great Is Thy Faithfulness." My prayer was for "new mercy, morning by morning." Believe me; you will need new mercy, morning by morning to deal with the unfortunate aftershocks of this seismic adventure called divorce.

When my former wife started dating...

I don't know what this aftershock measured on the emotional Richter scale, but I can tell you that it had produced major seismic activity. You know that it's bound to happen; but how can you prepare for it? The woman whom you love is now seeing someone else. I remember when I discovered that she was seeing someone. It was around Valentine's Day that I went to pick up my children; I saw the most beautiful vase full of lovely flowers. I had suspected that someone else was in the picture but just didn't want to accept it. However, when I saw the flowers I knew it! My heart felt like it had been pierced and my mouth grew dry. I was speechless. I don't know if she noticed the sudden change in my demeanor but believe me it changed. I had to go to the car and wait on the children.

I wanted to ask her some questions but didn't believe that it was my right. After all, she was single. It was not that she did anything wrong. The divorce was final and she was a free woman. The problem was within me. I was still holding out for hope; but now hope seemed lost.

I didn't want to be hypocritical. I too had a friend and she certainly had that same right. But when I saw evidence of it, it was like an elephant had fallen on me. My God what an aftershock!

I had a plethora of inquiries. Who is this guy? Do the children know about this? Is he a decent guy? All of these questions went through my mind. I wouldn't dare ask my children anything about it because I didn't know how much they knew and didn't feel that it was my right to tell them. Secondly, I'm old fashioned and just don't believe in involving children in "GROWN FOLK BUSINESS." I think that we do a major disservice to them, particularly in their developmental stage.

Finally, the identity of this mystery guy was revealed to me and for some reason I was comfortable with the decision. I felt that at least she chose a seemingly nice guy. This was just an inescapable fact that aftershocks follow an earthquake. There are also many other aftershocks that I could have shared with you but I just wanted to touch some of the major ones. In fact, your aftershocks may be altogether different than what I experienced.

The earthquake shakes and loosens the foundation, and the aftershocks can bring the structure to the ground. This is the normal pattern when one goes through the process of a divorce. But God! That's a mouth full. Whenever you go through any tough and trying experience, always factor God in it.

I say this because I went through the earthquake and the aftershocks and probably should not have made it but

GOD was with me. David expressed it well in Psalms 23: *"Yea though I walk through the valley of the shadow of death I will fear no evil because God is with me."* That's a "BUT GOD" right there!

I would encourage anyone going through or having been through a divorce or any earth-shattering event in life to make sure that you have a relationship with God. The fact is that many people never recover from the affects of divorce but I did and continue to do so. You too can recover, and just like I did, you will learn some valuable lessons in the process. The most important factor is simply learning how to TRUST GOD completely.

Chapter Eight

TRUSTING GOD

C hristian hymnals have entire sections of songs devoted to the theme of "TRUST." And of course, the Bible commentaries devote much discussion to the subject as well. In the African American Church, there is a favorite old hymn entitled, "I Will Trust in the Lord." But, exactly what is trust?

I like the definition made available in Webster's Dictionary which identifies trust in this manner:

"To place confidence; to commit or place in one's care or keeping"

Trust occurs when I can place what I have or who I am in the hands of someone else for safekeeping. Trust is in force when you sit on a bench and believe that it will hold you. It is like driving over a bridge and knowing that it will not collapse. Trust is like standing on a ladder and believing that it will not break.

For me to trust someone with my possessions is one thing, but to trust someone with my life is another. Of course, there is a difference in one's possessions and one's life. My possessions could be my car, clothes, or home. Lost possessions can be replaced or regained. In contrast, my life, simply put, is my life. It's me, who I am and all that I am.

There have been many times when I have allowed a car detailer to come to pick up my most expensive automobile for cleaning. Was I concerned? Yes, I was. However, I found solace in the fact that even if lost, stolen, or damaged, the automobile could be repaired or replaced. My life and my emotions are a whole different story.

I used to play a little game with my son when he was very small. I would toss him into the air and catch him. I remember how he would laugh and enjoy that little game. I thought about it years later and realized how potentially dangerous that could have been. I also thought about how my son must have had considerable trust in me to allow me, and in fact, ask me to toss him into the air. He placed trust in me because I was his father and he knew that I loved him. He developed the trust and felt confident that I would do whatever I had to do in order to keep him from harm. That is the kind of trust that I want to talk about; not trust in people but trust in God. It can be described as BLIND TRUST. My son placed trust in me because he believed in my ability to catch him when he began to fall.

It is a known fact that for those of us who love and know God, we develop a greater level of trust during difficult times. That was certainly true for me. If I can claim any good from my divorce, it is that it forced me into a position where I continued to learn more daily about the God I serve. It was at this point, after years of ministering to others, I could truly trust Him.

One of the most beautiful things about being a Christian is that you have a relationship with Jesus, God's son. As Christians, we believe that we can communicate directly with God through His Son. It is through this communication that our relationship is strengthened. It was through the strength of this relationship that my level of trust was raised. It was necessary to continue this trust on an even greater level when it felt as though God was not hearing my prayer. Like the experience with my son, I felt as though I had been tossed high into the air; and like him, I had faith in my FATHER to catch me before I hit bottom.

I've been privileged to study the Scripture extensively. In doing so, I've learned about the omnipotence of God. I am fully aware that He is awesome and all powerful. Through His power we discover that He is also most reliable. Because of an established relationship, we have access to an all-powerful being. We can trust and rely on His omnipotence. That's good news to me because it gives me a sense of security through the turbulent times in my life. Believe me, when I tell you, I've had some of those times. I have encountered many difficulties of life, but going through the period of divorce was one of the worst and most difficult.

Unequivocally, I made it and am making it because I developed complete trust in God.

DEVELOPING THIS TRUST...

The kind of trust that I relied upon did not just happen. It had to be developed over a period of time. Babies are born with a fear of falling and insecurity. I used the example of my son and the trust he developed in me to prevent him from hitting the ground or the floor. The first time I tossed him into the air he was frightened. It was only after he was conscious of the fact that I had not only the ability to catch him but total determination to do so. After a while, when he was old enough to recognize me and know that my hands and arms were gentle and meant him no harm, he abandoned all fear and replaced it with great anticipation of what his father could do and the joy I could deliver.

In other words, trust must be developed. Just because you are a Christian, and have subscribed or ascribed to the ways of Christ, doesn't mean that you truly trust God. Sadly, there are many in the body of Christ who exhibit very little trust. This is because at the time of salvation they did not fully draw from a well of privilege. Initially, you received the saving grace of God. Trusting in God fully must be developed over a period of time just as Clinton, Jr. grew to trust me.

It is a process and comes over time and through tests. It would be a great thing if we accepted all that we need at the point of salvation, but we know that's not the case. Of course, that's not the fault of God. When I was saved I received all of Him. The problem is that He did not get all of me. One of the things He didn't get was my full ability or willingness to trust him. I had to develop trust because of the burdens that were too overwhelming for me to bear under my own strength.

How Does One Develop Trust?

There are many ways to develop trust in God. I developed trust through **TEACHING, TRIALS, and TIME.**

- First of all, we learn to trust God by being open to **sound teaching**.
- After we have been taught and trials come, we then learn to trust God through these **trials**. It's like using certain muscles. Our strength increases as we strategically make use of them. Trials can also place you in a state of uncertainty and reduce you to a sense of helplessness and surrender.

- Coming to the end of your resources will cause you to learn patience, abandon the idea of being fully in control of your life, and will enhance the ability to wait on God. This I will call **time**. Let's look at each factor separately:

Trust through Teaching

Let us first address the importance of teaching. One of the real problems in the Christian community is the attitude that we have when it comes to teaching. When we talk about trusting God we will discover that teaching is the most important element. Teaching sustains us while we experience two additional elements – **trials and time**. I develop trust in God through my continuous study of His word. Paul said to Timothy, *"Study to show yourself approved unto God."*

Jesus taught His disciples so that they would be prepared for impending danger designed to destroy them. In His teaching, He shared that life would not be easy – even for the Christian. He reminded them that they would be exposed as sheep among wolves. But it was through exposure to continued teaching that they were conditioned and learned that He would be with them always even until the end of the earth.

It is incumbent upon me to share this fundamental need to be taught; especially if you are the one going through a divorce or some other catastrophic situation. While I was going through, I was able to draw from a well of teaching and scriptural reinforcement. I reviewed many lessons that I learned before the trouble, before the trials, and before the tribulations. Can I suggest something to you? I speak now not as a preacher/pastor but as one who has become a student of the word. Stay in church! Stay in Sunday school! Stay in Bible class! The helpful truths that you will learn will be essential as you go through the complex times in your life.

I saved this Scripture for last to really illustrate that it is through teaching that I developed trust in God. You probably know it already. *"Faith comes by hearing and hearing by the word of God."* I enjoy reading and studying the Scriptures from the New Living Translation of the Bible. When I read this passage from this version it really illuminated my mind concerning faith and trust coming by way of teaching. Let's examine this modern translation:

"Yet faith comes from listening to this message of good news, the Good News about Christ."

We all know that FAITH and TRUST are synonymous; which means that they are similar and very closely related. Like a versatile garment, they are somewhat reversible or interchangeable. Faith means trust and trust means faith. Since I increase faith by hearing, then I increase trust by hearing the word of God.

Have you ever looked at someone's situation and said that you couldn't imagine how they made it through? You might have said, "If I had to go through what they went through I probably would have lost my mind." In fact, I had a dear friend to say to me, "Clinton, you are a strong man to still have your sanity with all you are going through." He continued, "If I had to deal with what you are dealing with I don't think that I could do it."

What he was referring to is what I call "spin-offs" from the divorce. Here is a natural illustration. The situation felt like the famous Hurricane Katrina that came through Mississippi, Louisiana, and Alabama. Most of the devastation came from the hurricane but other devastation came from tornados that were generated or spun-off as a result of the hurricane.

Unfortunately, that's how it was during this period of divorcement. As if the divorce was not bad enough, there were spin-offs from the tragedy or as I shared in the last chapter on "Aftershocks"—as in rumors and lies. This is why my friend was amazed that I appeared so strong because I was confronted with a plethora of issues that could have broken the strongest person. Even though broken, this is when I relied upon what I had been taught. I never will forget saying to myself, "You have told others about a God you can trust; now it's time to TRUST HIM yourself." It was in this process of divorce that I spiritually regurgitated all that I had learned. I used it to develop ultimate trust in God.

Trust through Trials

Secondly, we develop trust through **trials.**

"Count it all joy when you fall into divers temptations: Knowing this, that the trying of your faith works patience.

But let patience have her perfect work, that ye may be perfect and entire, wanting nothing."

The word temptation in this text connotes trials. It refers to those things in life that shake us when we least expect it.

The text above is found in the Book of James. Look at how it appears in the New Living Translation...

"Dear brothers and sisters, whenever trouble comes your way, let it be an opportunity for joy. For when your faith is tested, your endurance has a chance to grow. So let it grow, for when your endurance is fully developed, you will be strong in character and ready for anything."

In life, all of us will have trials. I have read this passage many times because it assures me that I can learn something from trials. All of our trials may not be the same because James talked about divers temptations or trials. The word "divers" means many different kinds. The situation that I'm dealing with in this book represents trial in the form of divorce. Of course you may be reading this book and divorce may not be your issue; but believe me, developing trust will work for any trying situation.

I must admit that I learned much more about trusting God through trials than I did through my time of peace. I will also be honest and admit that sometimes when things were going well in my life, I was not as conscious of the need to rely on God. I would go through my day and forget to pray or my prayers would be short and void of passion. But when I was faced with trials, I was compelled to trust the God whom I had preached about. I discovered a new level of reaching out to Him with all of my being—and with ongoing passion.

I don't want you to think that trials automatically cause you to develop a greater level of trust because I have seen people go through trials and become worse or faithless. I believe that it is how you handle your trials. The Scripture teaches that we should handle them with PATIENCE. What is patience?

Biblical patience is the ability to put up with. It is the same word that we find in the Bible called longsuffering. The meaning of longsuffering is self-defined. It is the ability to suffer long or to put up with something without collapsing or giving away. So, when I go through trials and I patiently deal with what I'm going through, I am compelled to develop a greater trust in God. The reason being is the only way that I can calmly and patiently go through what I am going through is with God's help.

Life dealt me a blow. I was emotionally, spiritually, and brutally kicked. As the old saying goes, **"When you are kicked, let it kick you forward."** That's the stance that I chose to accept.

Trust through Time

Finally, I discovered that trust can be developed over **time**. This is a difficult one because it causes you to have to wait. To wait, even on God, is a state in which most of us find little joy. By nature, we are impatient and restless. We are ready to move at our own pace. One of the things that I continue to learn about God is that, in spite of how we scream, cry, or yell, He moves at his own pace. Sometimes it seems to be painfully slow.

While I was going through the period of divorce, I wanted God to move a little more quickly in healing me or to resolve some, if not all, of the issues. I was hurting and was tired of dealing with the pain of being torn apart. It seemed as if the more I wanted God to move, the slower He became. There is a song whose lyrics state, *"God knows what is best for me although my weary eyes cannot see; so I'll just thank you Lord because I won't complain."* Well, that is certainly a true song. God moves at His own pace because he knows the pace of our development. In other words, He knows how long to leave us in the oven. **It is not God's purpose to instantly deliver us from the situation but to develop us in the situation. It is only then that He allows deliverance to occur.**

Among others, there is a well known biblical personality who was meticulously forced to learn about God working within His own time frame. When God carried him through the process, (which took many years), he understood that had God not taken him through this prolonged set of circumstances he would have made some awful mistakes. His name was Joseph.

He experienced a dream from God which revealed impending greatness, regality, and royalty. Naturally, Joseph thought that the dream would come to fruition very soon; but it didn't. Joseph had to go through many trials over an extended period of time. In fact it took over thirteen years for his dream to become a reality.

He went through a series of digressions. His blood brothers placed him in a pit and left him there to die. Because one of the brothers pleaded on his behalf, he was taken from the pit and sold to Potiphar who was a powerful man in Egypt. After being falsely accused by Potiphar's wife, he was then thrown into prison; but from the prison, he was elevated to the palace. Joseph rose to Second in Command in the kingdom of Egypt. It took time but everything God promised him that He would do, He indeed brought into manifestation. In other words, IT HAPPENED! Over the course of time he had developed immense trust in God.

Sometimes, God has to allow us to spend some time in some uncomfortable situations. It is when we spend time in these situations that our trust is strengthened.

Is this what I mean by trust? Yes, it is! OK, I will trust God because I can see the hand of God in this situation. That's what most of us will say. That's pretty good. It's good when you can finally acknowledge that you see the hand of God in a situation. But, there are times when regardless of your level of spirituality you won't immediately see God's hand working in your situation. What do I do then? The answer is simple. **You must TRUST Him when you can't TRACE Him.**

I went through a period when I felt forsaken by God. I felt as if God was punishing me for something that I had done. Then there were times when I felt that God was not punishing or blessing me. I felt nothing. I was numb. I felt that He was nowhere to be found. I'm glad to say that this feeling did not last long; but it did occur from time to time.

Sometimes we become blinded by our burdens. We can't see God in it and we certainly cannot trace Him. That's a sad state of being but it is a state that most of us at some point have found ourselves. As a Christian and a student of the word, I understand that:

- I must trust God anyhow and under ALL circumstances!
- I must trust Him when I can't trace Him!
- I must trust God when I can't feel Him!
- I must trust God when I can't touch Him!

- I must trust God when I can't hear Him but I know He's there!

The good news of the Scripture is that He will NEVER leave you nor forsake you. If I'm in a situation where I feel that God is not to be found, it is because **I** moved – **NOT** Him!

I felt it necessary to include this chapter about trust because whenever you go through the dissolution of a marriage, lack of trust is bound to surface. You have a problem trusting another person and even some of your friends. I must be honest with you; I got to the point where my level of trust was at an all-time low. Not only did I experience the dissolution of a marriage that I literally thought would never end, but I suffered through experiences with so-called friends who took this opportunity to back stab me. If there is anything that will inhibit your ability to trust, it is when people you thought you could trust and promised to never jeopardize your trust eventually then seek to betray or abandon you.

I only mention this because I do not want you to lose faith should you go through something similar. What I had to realize and be thankful for is that God is mercifully not like man. I praise Him for His steadfastness! Sometimes we have a tendency to distrust God because man is not trustworthy. Of course, I'm not talking about those of us who have grown to the point of totally trusting God, but I do realize that there are those who see God through their own frail, fickle, and finite frame of reference. God is BIGGER and BETTER!

When you are married to someone who promised to be with you for better or worse, richer or poorer, in sickness and health, and you face the fact that the vow has been broken; it affects your ability to trust. Trust is most significant and especially crucial to a relationship. My marital situation, of course, did not involve sickness or health, richer or poorer because we were truly blessed of God in those areas. We were not rich as it relates to Forbes Magazine standards and not even our neighbor's standards, but we had what we needed and most of what we desired. Well, maybe we were rich. I mean we had a nice home with all financial obligations paid on time, good health, and healthy children. In this sense, we were quite rich!

Our specific challenge became, "for better or worse." Believe me before it was all over, it seemed like there was little "better" and a lot of "worse." The fact remains that we made a vow before God and that vow was unfortunately broken. Did we have Biblical and legal grounds for a divorce? Yes! But even with grounds, your ability to trust is affected.

Trust is so important because many people whom I have spoken with or counseled have a problem contemplating remarrying. In fact, I had to deal with this myself. How could I trust the next person when, for whatever reason, I had been found undesirable and made to feel unwanted? Now I have learned that when we truly learn to trust God we trust Him to lead us to the right person. So, my trust should not be necessarily in the next person or the last person. Rather, it should be in God!

When I trust God I will be confident that regardless of the actions of the person whom I'm in a relationship with, God can handle both her and me. This is true for a spouse or a friend. This is so liberating because it can be a miserable and lonely life when you are plagued with the trust factor.

Should you trust again?

Yes, most definitely! You SHOULD trust again!

Can you trust again?

Sure, you CAN trust again!

Will you trust again?

Yes, you MUST trust again!

You must plant these thoughts into your spirit, "I WILL TRUST again because it is God whom I trust. I trust God to guide me and select the one for me." The Psalmist says, *"In thee oh Lord I put my trust."*

I HAVE DONE THAT! It happened on the other side of a dark and terrible wilderness experience.

Chapter Nine

HOW DOES THE BIBLE ADDRESS DIVORCE

There are many viewpoints on the issue of divorce in the Christian community. In this part of the book, I'd like to examine God's word to get a clear understanding of what He has to say about this crucial subject. I think that this is most important simply because there are varied opinions concerning this matter. Even when it comes to those of us who are Bible students and claim to derive our position from the Scriptures, there are a myriad of opinions, even among clergy. In fact, you can possibly identify fifty Bible scholars and theologians and assemble them in a room together for a week and have them study and discuss the biblical implications and treatment of divorce, and you would come out with just as many different opinions as there are people in the room. There is no wonder how confusing and distorted the whole matter has become.

I have read studies and listened to many scholars, preachers, and teachers as they have presented their views on the subject. In addition to this, I have conducted personal research using Scripture as a primary resource. I have also relied upon the dictates of culture and personal experiences. It is at this point that I shudder with responsibility because of my innate desire to not mislead any person reading this book. I don't claim to be an authority on this subject; however, I do feel anointed and appointed to discuss it. I have prayed and have sought God in the matter. At the end of the day, He continues to be our most reliable and most infallible resource. I would not even think about completing this work without giving what I believe is a Biblical view.

What I have discovered is there are many extreme beliefs on this subject. The wide range of differing opinions is nothing less than amazing. I have listened to those scholars who believe that a person should not divorce even under the most extreme circumstances. They often believe that it is God's will for you to stay in your marriage under threat, abuse, and even adultery.

I have personally been subjected to the school of thought that suggests that if you divorce and remarry that you can't live a life pleasing to God. You must leave the one you are with and go back to reconnect with your first spouse.

There are those who believe that if a person divorces and remarries, they are hell bound without question. Additionally, from personal and painful experience, I have been told that if a pastor is a divorcee then he is no longer qualified to hold this honorable and godly office. This is an extreme conservative view.

Then there are those who take a more liberal approach. I would probably describe this group as the "Anything Goes Theorists." They believe that divorce should be permitted in almost any circumstance. If you are no longer happy with your spouse, just leave them. If they gain weight and are not as attractive as they once were, just leave them. If he loses his job and is not able to financially support you in the manner that you are accustomed, just leave him. This liberal approach is one that is very selfish and not selfless.

It has no biblical foundation or support. It is built upon the premise that it is only about MY happiness and well being. It is sanctioned and addressed in the legal system. Thus, we have in this country a "No Fault Divorce."

As we continue in this chapter, you will discover that even Jesus was called upon for clarification and had to deal with this liberal approach with a group called the Pharisees. The Pharisees were the religious leaders of that day. This gives us to know that this approach is not just a modern day belief. There were many men in biblical days and times of antiquity that left their wives for the very least of reasons.

I have given you a brief synopsis of the extreme views. But the question is still on the table: "What does the Bible have to say about divorce?" After careful perusal of the actual words of Jesus, I have discovered that quantitatively he said little about divorce however qualitatively he said an awful lot. In other words, HIS few words carry a strong and powerful message. Let's examine HIS words.

It hath been said, Whosoever shall put away his wife, let him give her a writing of divorcement: But

I say unto you, That whosoever shall put away his wife, saving for the cause of fornication, causes her to commit adultery: and whosoever shall marry her that is divorced commits adultery. **Matthew 5:31-32 (KJV)**

In this Scripture, please note that Jesus is preaching to His disciples and followers in what has been identified in Bible history as the Sermon on the Mount. This often-referenced message is a discourse where Jesus shares many things with his followers. If you read it you will ascertain that it is an instructional message. Jesus felt called upon and taught this lesson in order to clear up many of the traditional beliefs that had been blown out of proportion or taken out of context.

In these next passages of Scripture, Jesus answers a question that was purposed by a group of men who came with the intention of trapping him with his own words. They knew already what he believed but they wanted to be combative and inject confusion. Let's examine how He handled the situation in these passages.

The Pharisees also came unto him, tempting him, and saying unto him, Is it lawful for a man to put away his wife for every cause? And he answered and said unto them, Have ye not read, that he which made them at the beginning made them male and female, and said, For this cause shall a man leave father and mother, and shall cleave to his wife: and they twain shall be one flesh? Wherefore they are no more twain, but one flesh. What therefore God hath joined together, let not man put asunder. They say unto him, why did Moses then command to give a writing of divorcement, and to put her away? He said unto them, Moses because of the hardness of your hearts suffered you to put away your wives: but from the beginning it was not so. And I say unto you, whosoever shall put away his wife, except it be for fornication, and shall marry commits adultery: and whoso marries her who is put away doth commit adultery. **Matthew 19:3-9 (KJV)**

I'm sure that you can already tell how Jesus feels about divorce. Earlier in this chapter, I shared my wonderment concerning Jesus' brevity on this very important subject. Through prayer, God gave me the answer. It is because God never meant for man and woman to divorce. If you notice in Jesus' response to the Pharisees, He spoke more about marriage although they asked about divorce. He said, *for this cause shall a man leave father and mother, and shall cleave to his wife: and they twain shall be one flesh? Wherefore they are no more twain, but one flesh. What therefore God hath joined together, let not man put asunder.*

Jesus' position aligns with what God said through the prophet Malachi. It is in Malachi that God states un-categorically that He HATES divorce. He totally despises the putting away of one's wife or husband. It is true that divorce was never God's idea. God ordained marriage from the beginning to be between one man and one woman. Marriage is a covenant agreement and it is meant for life.

We must also understand that just as divorce was not God's idea, sin also was not His idea. From the beginning, God's expectation for man is that he would live a sinless life. When God created this world he created the Garden of Eden. He then placed Adam and Eve in the garden. He created them with the capacity to live a sinless life. But as you know, very soon thereafter they messed up and found themselves well outside of His intentions for them. Because of this, God mercifully implemented a backup plan. In the case of sin he gave us Jesus. What we must understand is that Jesus' sojourn on earth was not God's best idea. God NEVER meant for His Son to come to this earth to die for man's sin. His earthly life represented an INTERVENTION! So then every time we think of Jesus we should think of our sin and thank God for the concessions made on our behalf.

Because He is our Creator, God is not surprised when we fail to fully honor His expectations. With tremendous compassion He makes allowances for us through merciful concessions.

His concessions were not as liberal as the Pharisaic view but as we can tell from the text, there are some instances when God, in His permissive but not perfect will, will allow or maybe a better description would be "tolerate" divorce. It is well worth it to note that God NEVER COMMANDS divorce but again, there are some instances where He will permit it. It is important to recognize this difference because the Pharisees took God's word given to Moses out of context concerning divorce. Look once again at what they said:

They say unto him, why did Moses then command to give a writing of divorcement, and to put her away? **Matthew 19:7 (KJV)**

So was it a Command? Moses NEVER commanded anyone to get a divorce. Let's see what position is actually attributed to Moses under the inspiration of God.

When a man hath taken a wife, and married her, and it come to pass that she find no favor in his eyes, because he hath found some uncleanness in her: then let him write her a bill of divorcement, and give it in her hand, and send her out of his house. **Deut. 24:1 (KJV)**

The word in the text is not "command." Notice that Moses said "LET him write her a bill of divorcement." They took God's instructions to Moses out of context. It is not an unusual case for the impure and unholy to seek justification of their conduct from the law of God itself, and to adjust or manipulate Scripture to their own destruction. It is obvious that divorce was their carnal desire. Normally, when we want to do a thing that is contrary to command, we will take the command out of context.

If you will now notice that Jesus never did address the fact that they said Moses commanded that we give her a letter of divorcement. He went on to explain the rationale behind what Moses said. Look at Jesus' reply:

Moses permitted divorce as a concession to your hard-hearted wickedness, but it was not what God had originally intended. **Matthew 19:8 (NLT)**

Please remember that Moses got his orders from God. What is Jesus talking about when he says, *"Your hard-hearted wickedness?"* We don't totally understand why Jesus said that they were hard-hearted but we do know that obviously there was something going on in Moses' day that would move God to instruct Moses to permit divorce. The term hard-hearted signals a serious emotional deficit or an extremely rigid stance or state of being. In itself, it is worth close examination and evidently warranted the attention of God Himself. Moses dealt with the undeniable presence of hard-hearted spirits. Feeling completely handicapped and unable to change the mind of these cold and determined individuals, he made allowances in what he considered a life and death situation for many women especially.

Moses perceived that if divorce were not permitted, in many cases, the women would be exposed to great hardships through the cruelty of their husbands. There were many men in that day who had become disgruntled with their wives and because divorce, prior to Moses' instructions in Deuteronomy 24, was not even practiced, when they had no more affection for their wives they were then harshly treated. Some theologians and early scholars said that women were "coming up missing" or killed just because men were tired of them and had no way out of the marriage.

In the New Testament, Jesus admitted that divorce was allowed, but still it was his contention that this was far from God's original design and purpose of marriage.

Divorce was only a temporary expedient growing out of a special state of emotional failures and not designed to be perpetual. He considered the unfortunate hardness of the hearts of those involved at the time. In other words, divorce became a convenient "Plan B" or escape hatch for hard-hearted men with wives who had done no wrong, however their husbands just wanted to be rid of them.

By the time we get to Malachi, the last book of the Old Testament and four hundred years before the writings of Matthew, divorce had become so commonplace until God was moved in disgust and voiced such sentiment in what has been translated as, "I hate divorce!"

Jesus addresses the matter in Matthew. It was at that time that God had become so frustrated with the actions and inactions of his people until He did not speak to them for 400 years. So, by the time that the Pharisees addressed Jesus with this question, the concessions, which Moses had originally delivered from God, had been so misconstrued and distorted until divorce was allowed for any and every reason.

Let's look again at the Pharisees inquiry:

Is it lawful for a man to put away his wife for every cause? **Matthew 19:3 (KJV)**

Notice a couple of things in this 3rd verse. The verse states that the Pharisees came to Jesus "tempting" him. As used in this passage, "tempting" means to test. The New Living Translation of the Bible says that they came trying to "trap" Jesus. They tried to trap him with the fact that there were two general beliefs about divorce. The conservative belief was that the only reason one could divorce was for the sake of adultery. The liberal belief was that a man could divorce his wife for any reason. He was to give her a writing of divorcement stating that they were once married but now there was dissolution of the marriage. She was now free to remarry. The second thing I want you to look at are the words EVERY CAUSE. Those who challenged Jesus asked Him "What does the law say about a man leaving his wife for any reason?"

Both groups were standing around waiting for an answer from Jesus. He responded to the inquiry by taking them back to the beginning:

And he answered and said unto them, Have ye not read, that he which made them at the beginning made them male and female, And said, For this cause shall a man leave father and mother, and shall cleave to his wife: and they twain shall be one flesh? Wherefore they are no more twain, but one flesh. What therefore God hath joined together, let not man put asunder. **Matthew 19:4-6 (KJV)**

Looking at Jesus' response, it's very clear. I must repeat myself when I say that God meant for a man and a woman to come together in holy matrimony, cleave to each other, and become one flesh. When this occurs it was to be a life-long commitment. Since they are no longer two but one, let no one separate them. God has joined them together.

In the Old Testament, we found God entering into a state of concession for the sake of man. Here, in the New Testament we find Jesus making similar concessions. We see it in His teaching on divorce in the sermon that emanated from the Mount of Olives. We also see it in his response to the inquiry of the Pharisees. That concession is in the case of fornication. Notice His words,

But I say unto you, that whosoever shall put away his wife, saving for the cause of fornication, causes her to commit adultery.

Notice that Jesus uses the word fornication in both texts. Exactly **what is fornication?** Simply stated, it is simply sex outside of the bonds of holy matrimony and connotes any kind of ungodly sexual act. The Greek word for fornication in this text is the word porneia (por-ni'-ah). It is where we get our English word pornography. Pornography, according to Merriam-Webster's dictionary is the *"depiction of erotic behavior intended to cause sexual excitement."* When you study the word fornication, you will find that it is adultery but it includes all sexual acts outside of the bonds of holy matrimony. It includes prostitution, molestation, homosexuality, incest and much more. God does not want us going to strip clubs, viewing pornographic images and filling our minds with all kinds of lustful images. When this occurs it is a violation of the marriage vows.

So is fornication the only reason given in Scripture that warrants a divorce? I must be very careful when I address this question because I don't ever want to take Scripture out of context. There is another passage that we find in 1 Corinthians where the Apostle Paul addresses divorce. Look at his teaching:

Now, for those who are married I have a command that comes not from me, but from the Lord. A wife must not leave her husband. But if she does leave him, let her remain single or else go back to him. And the husband must not leave his wife. **1 Cor. 7:10-11 (NLT)**

Notice that he says that this commandment comes from God. Here again, it is very clear that God was totally against divorce.

He then addresses divorce in the case of one of the spouses being a non-believer. When they were married initially, neither of them was Christian; but now one has heard the gospel message and has converted, but the other spouse did not convert. Of course this makes it very difficult for the spouse who is now a Christian. So the question

was raised concerning whether or not they could divorce.
Look at Paul's response in this matter.

*Now, I will speak to the rest of you, though I do not
have a direct command from the Lord. If a Christian
man has a wife who is an unbeliever and she is willing
to continue living with him, he must not leave her.
And if a Christian woman has a husband who is an
unbeliever, and he is willing to continue living with
her, she must not leave him. For the Christian wife
brings holiness to her marriage, and the Christian
husband brings holiness to his marriage. Otherwise,
your children would not have a godly influence, but
now they are set apart for him. (But if the husband
or wife who isn't a Christian insists on leaving,
let them go. In such cases the Christian husband
or wife is not required to stay with them, for God
wants his children to live in peace.) You wives must
remember that your husbands might be converted
because of you. And you husbands must remember
that your wives might be converted because of you.*
1 Cor. 7:12-16 (NLT)

The concession here is abandonment. It's very clear that the believer must not leave the unbeliever just because he or she is not a Christian; but in contrast, if the unbeliever chooses to leave the believer for any reason then Paul says that the believer should permit it.

Why then did this Scripture not permit the believer to leave the unbeliever? Paul said it in that 16th verse. You wives must remember that your husbands might be converted because of you, and you husbands must remember that your wives might be converted because of you. The goal of the Christian, even in the worst of situations, is to win a soul.

Are there other concessions?

I have tried to bring attention to every Scripture that speaks of divorce in the Bible. From reading these Scriptures I can't stress it too much: God hates divorce! If God hates it then we who are His followers should also hate it. Although God hates it, we still see that there were some concessions made. He instructed Moses to make a concession and Jesus gave us the reason why: because of their hardened hearts. Paul was instructed under the inspiration of the Holy Spirit to allow it in the case of a non-believer who left a believer. Even Jesus made a concession in the case of fornication or adultery.

If there were concessions made then based upon the desire of some who were just not willing to do right in the marriage then what about now? I know that this is something that the church does not want to deal with but because 50% of all Christian first marriages end in divorce, we must deal with it!

Allow me now to share with you what I now believe. When I speak of what I believe I'm talking about my basic beliefs according to the heart of God. My stance is based upon personal study of God's heart in totality. I believe that you can really get to know a person's heart by listening to what he or she says. I have been a student of God's word and have tried to look at God not just from isolated statements but from reading his total word.

During the worst times of being in a divorce, I needed and sought compassion from some people, even my friends in the clergy who discontinued being in relationship with me. One of the things that I have learned about God is that He is a **compassionate** God. He is **loving** and **kind**.

God understands that though He has set and prescribed laws, there are people who will violate those laws who will sometimes prompt the actions of others involved to protect and care for themselves. For instance, God said, "Thou shall not kill" but does allow one to protect himself in the event that his life is threatened.

It's true; God hates divorce, but living in a real world as we know it today, should the person who is in an abusive and dangerous relationship remain in a painful and life-threatening situation? If you are married to a person who is involved in some illegal activity that could potentially be hazardous to your life and the life of your children and family, should you stay? If, when you come home and before you get a hello, you are confronted with a fist, should you stay?

There are so many other scenarios that I could list at this point. I must be bold and deal with it because this is a reality in so many lives.

As a pastor and spiritual counselor, my question has always been, "Are these people who are the innocent victims of this kind of activity sentenced to a life of misery because it seems that they have no Biblical grounds for divorce? Should a wife, for the sake of our beliefs, just wait until her husband kills her? Should a husband constantly live under the threat of hot boiling grits?"

I know what some would say. A person should not leave if it is not a Biblical reason. However, my question is if God allowed some concession based upon certain situations in biblical times, then what about now?

Please allow me to restate my position. I believe, as Jesus intimated, God never commanded divorce; but it was permitted. I do believe that there are many divorces that occur in the Christian community that are certainly not warranted. I certainly am not attempting to give anyone a way out of their marriage simply because they're not happy anymore. However, if there are some areas of violation which pose certain danger or emotional destruction, then it is up to you to make the call. There are also those instances where an individual desires with all their heart to remain in a marriage; however, their spouse absolutely refuses to continue the relationship.

I certainly don't want us to be like some of the Pharisees who would leave their wives just because they gained weight and were no longer the shapely hourglass "36-24-

36" that they married. I also cannot become an advocate for individuals who feel that one has grounds to leave their spouse because they're not happy anymore or they are not pleased with them anymore. Those are all selfish reasons. In deep perusal of the Scriptures, I cannot justify or align my opinion with such selfish dismissals.

I know of a situation where a woman left her husband simply because she was not happy with her life and blamed it on the fact that she was married to the wrong guy. She later discovered that her problem was not with the person that she saw in the window but the one in the mirror. That's a selfish reason.

Here again, if you are in a situation wherein your marriage is not what it should be, PLEASE SEEK CHRISTIAN COUNSEL. If you are in a situation where you are being violated, I'm still not suggesting that you divorce as your first option. Pray first that God will give you strength to handle the situation and that He will change your spouse for the better. I have seen God do this!

I remember talking to a woman who had been married for 40 plus years. She shared with me that in the beginning of her marriage life was good, but a few years later her husband started committing adultery on a regular basis. She talked about how this made her feel less than a woman to know that her husband was enjoying the pleasures of another woman.

I asked the question, "How and why did you stay with him?"

She expressed the fact that so many times she thought about leaving him, but because he was a wonderful father, a good provider, and a very kind man she stayed with him. She said, "I realized that even with this problem that he had, he still had much good in him. So I prayed for God to give me strength and to straighten him out."

She then said to me with a smile, "And God did it. He is now at home every night and is faithful to me, and I have enjoyed many wonderful years with him now simply because I waited him out."

In summary, the Bible has a great deal to say about divorce and in certain instances. God Himself and Jesus have made concessions. Review of the word reveals:

1. Marriage is God's Idea and His Holy Institution
2. His Perfect Plan was that Man and Woman (Husband and Wife) would be joined for Life
3. Out of Compassion, He made certain concessions
4. He NEVER COMMANDED divorce, rather he ALLOWED it.
5. He understands our weakness and failure to fully live up to His expectations
6. His plan of redemption will not send you to hell or disqualify you as His child because you are divorced.

Chapter Ten

TRY! TRY AGAIN!

C onsidering marriage after a divorce can be a most frightening experience. Some individuals emerge so wounded and discouraged that they are unwilling to contemplate exposing their emotions to the same kind of vulnerability again—ever!

While I do not advise anyone to rush out and connect with the first person they might meet or date, I STRONGLY encourage individuals to make sure they leave open at least the option to love again—and more importantly, the option TO BE LOVED again. I also strongly recommend allowing a time of inner healing and forgiveness before moving forward.

Remember, this idea of companionship (male and female) was first God's idea. After creating the universe then man and woman, marriage became His first estab-lished institution. Evidently, He gave the matter great thought. I examined closely the thought process described in Genesis:

And the Lord God said, "It is not good for the man to be alone. I will make a companion who will help him." So, the Lord God caused Adam to fall into a deep sleep. He took one of Adam's ribs and closed up the place from which he had taken it. Then the Lord God made a woman from the rib and brought her to Adam.

And Adam said, "This is now bone of my bones, and flesh of my flesh. She shall be called Woman, because she was taken out of Man." Therefore, shall a man leave his father and his mother, and shall cleave unto his wife: and they shall be one flesh.

In this excerpt out of the Genesis account, we see the first **"not-good"** evaluation or assessment. As God created the universe, He looked at each phase of His work and said, **"It is good."**

- When God divided the land from the sea, he looked at it and said, **"It is good."**

- When God spoke to the ground and the ground brought forth every sort of grass and seed-bearing plants and trees, He looked at it and said, **"It is good."**

- When God spoke to the firmament and said, let bright lights appear in the sky to separate the day from the night. The greater one, the sun, presides during the day; the lesser one, the moon, presides through the night; He looked at it and said, **"It is good."**

- Then God said, "Let the waters swarm with fish and other life. Let the skies be filled with birds of every kind." Therefore, God created great sea creatures and every sort of fish and every kind of bird; He then looked at it and said, **"It is good."**

- God said, "Let the earth bring forth every kind of animal, livestock, small animals and wildlife." And, so it was. God made all sorts of wild animals, livestock and small animals, each able to reproduce more of its own kind. He looked at it and said, **"It is good."**

Then God said, Let us make man in our image, after our likeness: and let them have dominion over the fish of the sea, and over the fowl of the air, and over the cattle, and over all the earth, and over every creeping thing that creeps upon the earth. Therefore, God created man in his own image.

God observed man in the garden and saw that something about his situation appeared unfinished. He felt a strong sense of incompleteness. Here His human creation was in the garden with all of the blessings one could desire. (Remember, that God first created a paradise and then He created man and placed him in the midst of this very beautiful place). He was careful to provide His human creation with every material need his heart could desire. Then, God realized that man was ALONE and consequently lonely and without companionship. He then decided that man's loneliness was definitely NOT GOOD. Here in this flowing and poetic Genesis account we find an interruption of the **"It-is-good"** pattern.

Of course, through God's plan for creation, man had fowl, fish, horses, primates, and every imaginable creature to befriend. However, though animals can become great pets and sources of companionship, it was not God's plan for them to take the place of a suitable companion. Again, let me remind you that man had all of the material possessions one could desire. You must understand that at the time Adam was the first and only man, which means that the whole world was his as a gift. What a treat! What an opportunity! Initially however, he was still ALONE.

I have discovered that material blessings, no matter how plentiful, cannot provide everything you need or want for that matter. For example, a career is a great pursuit; reaching your retirement goal is admirable; a mortgage-free home is a great accomplishment but these things, within themselves, do not bring completeness or lasting joy.

Unfortunately, there are those who are so intrigued with what they have only to discover that achievement, personal gains, and other acquisitions cannot and will not fill that void designated for a SUITABLE mate, a human being. Ultimately, man needed someone who was compatible at the human level. Therefore, the Lord God caused

Adam to fall into a deep sleep. He then performed the first operation.

He took one of Adam's ribs and closed up the place from which He had taken it. Then the Lord God made a woman from the rib and brought her to Adam. Adam now discovered that this was the entity missing from his life equation. He immediately realized this inadequacy and said, *"This is now bone of my bones, and flesh of my flesh. She shall be called Woman, because she was taken out of Man."*

Adam's realization represents the compatibility that we all endeavor to have. It is fulfilling to live with someone whom you know was created just for you. This of course does not mean that when an individual seems created just for you that there will be no challenges. The Genesis account tells us that Adam and Eve had their challenges. Their challenges were so serious until they triggered eternal consequences. In fact, all of humanity suffers somewhat because of the mistakes of the first couple. However, even with challenges, misunderstandings and wrong-doings, to have someone whom you know is your SOUL-MATE or that special someone is one of the most fulfilling human emotions imaginable.

After my divorce, I discovered how lonely and alienating this unwelcomed status could be. Oh, I had the companionship of friends and peers; however, there was this new and nagging sense of loneliness. There was nothing in my closet, my home or my bank account that in any way served as a substitute. Sometimes my friends and I would go out and have dinner or engage in some other activities. I mentioned earlier that my brother stuck close by me and tried to make sure that the whole matter did not get the best of me. While I will always be grateful for his attention and brotherly love, it did not take the place of having someone in your life that you knew God made just for you. I longed for INTIMACY; not of a sexual nature but of a "blending-of-two-souls" nature. Day by day I walked with the emotional malady of a missing rib. The pain was excruciating.

Please understand that though I was alone and lonely I was not in a rush to reconnect because I understood the need to heal and to be COMPLETE ALONE. However, I share the fact that I was lonely and missing intimacy because it was a reality, and I knew that God had someone just for me.

Notice, God took woman out of man. This made Adam and Eve a perfect fit. I believe that for everyone who desires to be married there is a perfect mate waiting. Of course, it takes time, prayer and other efforts to find them or to be found, but believe me they are there.

The process also involves great patience. One of the worst things that we can do is to move ahead or accelerate faster than God. Sometimes we pray and believe God for a suitable mate and because God seems too slow, we take things into our own hands.

It is important that you realize and accept God's desire for His children to live a full and abundant life. For most, this may well mean living with a marriage partner created to uniquely make you happy and bless your life. At least, that is what God intended initially. I caution you to let Him have His perfect way in your life by believing Him to bring it all to pass in your life. **In your hurt and recovery, I advise you not to close doors that He has opened and not to open doors that He has closed.** Seek His face as to which doors He has opened as opposed to doors that serve as mere distractions.

It is dangerous not to wait on God. God moves in His own time because he knows what is best for us and the best time to give to us what we desire and need. Now I realize every time I have made a total wreck of my life I tried to help God out. The old saying is true, **"He is God all by Himself. He doesn't need anyone else."** I am certainly not the first individual who has tried to give God some help.

The book of Genesis also records the story of God's promise of a son to Abraham and Sarah. A seeming curse within itself, Sarah was barren during the years that she should have been fertile. By the time the story was recorded the years of childbearing were long past and yet the promise had not been fulfilled. At first, Abraham and Sarah believed God and waited patiently. They knew that if God said it, He was certainly able to bring it to pass. Years passed by but there was no development in the womb and no symptoms of an impending pregnancy – no morning sickness, no physical changes in her body's appearance, no child! Sarah desperately wanted a son for Abraham, the man she reverenced as her "lord." (Note: The lower case "l" does not signify divinity as much as it indicates the high respect as a woman displayed for a man she deeply appreciated). She wanted a male child to carry on the family name and receive the family's inheritance. Then, she came up with what she perceived as a bright idea. The plan involved her young maid whose name was Hagar. She conferred with Abraham concerning fathering a child with Hagar then she and Abraham could raise him as if he was their own.

I have read this particular passage many times and have found no objection on the part of Abraham. He obviously thought that this too was a good idea. Dying without an heir posed a nightmare that stared him in the face daily.

What a mistake! This turned out to be a painful decision because eventually God did just what He said concerning a son for Abraham and Sarah. When Isaac, THEIR SON was born, jealousy and strife found their way into his household. Ishmael, Hagar's son, started to harass and make fun of Isaac, Sarah's son.

To put the matter to rest, Abraham had to put his own son and Hagar, the maidservant, out of his dwelling. What a painful experience this must have been as Abraham severed ties with his own flesh and blood. This sad state of affairs occurred because of their inability or willingness to wait patiently on God's time.

Many people have lived, not in holy matrimony, but through hellacious matrimony only because of similar inability or unwillingness to wait on God's timing. Remember as I said before, God sometimes moves quickly and sometimes slowly to the point we don't feel the progression until it is complete. It is a part of His Sovereignty. Whether He moves quickly or slowly, it is important for us to wait until He says it is all right.

I was preaching at a church in a certain city where I had a conversation with an older woman who had married only two years prior. I had preached a sermon on God's timing and how necessary it is to wait for Him. She heard the message and shared her testimony with me at the conclusion of the service. She shared with me how happy she was and how God had blessed her with her SOUL MATE. Here was a woman who was educated and successful but went for many years living in an unmarried state. She wanted to be married and have children but none of the relationships developed to the point of marriage. She had high standards and people told her that she would never get married because she was too "picky."

She prayed during her twenties, thirties, forties and well into her fifties. She was smart, beautiful and successful, but still had no husband. One day, still in her fifties, she met a man who seemed as if he had dropped from heaven. They dated for a short while and then were married. I never will forget what she told me as I observed her face glowing like the sun. She said, "I had to wait for many years while watching some of my friends marry. I was happy for them but hurting inside because I wanted someone for me. As I look back now at some of my friends' marriages I am saddened because some of them have divorced, some have lived in abusive situations, and some have dealt with extramarital relationships on the part of their spouses. In retrospect, I thank God because I would rather marry the right one in my fifties than to have lived with the wrong man in my twenties, thirties and forties."

I believed that marriage was in God's plan for my life. Of course, I am not of the opinion that everyone has to be married. There are some individuals with the gift of celibacy who, for one reason or the other, have chosen to live peaceably in the unmarried state with reasonable content and satisfaction. Paul speaks about this in his writings on relationships. However, I believe that there is a larger group of individuals, including me, who fare much better in a marriage relationship.

I had people suggest to me that because I was free that I should just enjoy my life, and so to speak, "play the field." Then, there were some who suggested that because of the difficulty of my former marriage, the hurt and pain surrounding my divorce and the fact that divorce indicated failure or lack of capacity to maintain a stable relationship that I should not try again; but I remained optimistic. I held on to the hope that God would provide the companionship that my soul desired. Those of us who believe that marriage is for us should not allow the difficulty of an earlier marriage to hinder us from entering into it again.

We all face some areas of difficulty. We can all look back and find reasons or circumstances that could have caused us to consider giving up hope. However, something sustained us. Indeed, going through life was difficult, but we did not give up hope. Raising children was difficult, but we did not give up hope. I did not let the difficulty of anything cause me to be afraid to try again! Thankfully, I had the privilege to HEAL. I am grateful for this process because during this time I discovered that the dream of being whole and in a loving relationship could be totally revived.

I remember feeling the devastation when I could no longer deny the demise of my former marriage. I said to myself, "I tried it and I failed." Some of the failing was self-inflicted, and some was not of my doing. However, failing is failing. Some people would still classify me as a failure as a marriage partner today. Are they right? I don't think so!

Thank God, I have learned that failing is not failure unless you view it as failure. We have all failed at one thing or another. It might be a marriage, career, or business but a single isolated incident of failure does not make you a total failure.

I am a huge sports fan, and I remember when Barry Bonds broke Henry Aaron's home run record. I followed what came to be known as "THE CHASE" all that year. I watched how, time after time, Barry Bonds would knock the ball out of the park and come closer to the record. Barry Bonds was a baseball success. He eventually broke Henry Aaron's home run record, which made him the new home run king. He has more home runs than anyone including Aaron, Ruth, and Maris. What we usually do not look at is that Barry Bonds failed quite often. One thing I also discovered is how many times he would strike out, groundout, or fly out. To score an OUT indicates a temporary failure to get on base. However, Barry Bonds will not go down in sports history as a failure by any means, yet his record is not without shortcomings. I took a look at some of his statistics. I found them most interesting:

- At the time that he hit his 762nd home run, he had been at bat 9,844 times. Out of those 9,844 times at bat, he only had 2,935 hits.
- He was thrown out at the base 5,370 times

- He struck out 1,539 times, which gave him a batting average of .298.

The great Home Run King successfully hit the ball only three out of ten times, yet he is credited with the title of a super star. His stats support the position that he failed more than he succeeded, but he is still the Home Run Champion.

Life is like that. You do not have to live a life void of mistakes to be successful or a champion. **You have heard it before, "If at first you don't succeed, then try and try again."** The fact of the matter is that you will not live life void of mistakes and failure. Failing is a part of succeeding. May I go on to suggest to you that one who has never failed has also probably never succeeded.

Let me share this with you as I address failing or the desire to avoid failure: **There is only one way that you will go through life without failing and that is if you never try anything.** You become a failure when you allow your failing to stop you from ever trying again. Secondly, failing is not always a bad thing; it is HOW YOU LOOK AT IT. That is the way it is with most situations.

How do you view your situation? One can look at lemons and anticipate bitterness while another can taste tantalizing lemonade. One will look at a rosebush and see thorns and another can see and smell fragrant flowers. It is how you look at it—a matter of perception. For greater clarity, I offer another example. A few years ago, I preached a sermon on Elisha and his young student.

Elisha was an Old Testament prophet who found himself surrounded by the enemy. The king of Syria had dispatched soldiers to capture Elisha and bring him back to Syria. Elisha was a threat to the Syrian army because God had given him a supernatural gift. He was able to spy on the Syrians and reveal their plans of attack concerning Elisha's people in Israel. What was going on? Every time the king of Syria would dispatch a group of soldiers to do battle in a certain region of Israel, Elisha would tell the king of Israel the Syrian's plan.

Early one morning Elisha's young servant walked out of the house and to his dismay, he saw hundreds of soldiers surrounding the house ready to take Elisha into captivity. He ran to wake up Elisha. After waking up, Elisha walked out to investigate the young man's claim. The young servant was right! There were soldiers with horses and chariots surrounding the house. After watching the soldiers for a while, Elisha walked back into the house as if nothing was wrong.

The servant was confused. "Elisha," he said, "Do you not see the imminent danger we are in?" Elisha made a profound statement. He said, "Yes I see the horses, chariots, and men, *but there is more for us than for them.*"

What we must understand is that the servant could not see what Elisha (who had been in this situation before) could see. Elisha looked past the trouble and saw triumph. He looked past the DILEMMA and saw DELIVERANCE.

It is how you look at it. How do you view your failed marriage? How do you view your shattered dreams? If you view it as failure then you will not want to try again. If you view it as just a MINOR setback or a MAJOR setup for a comeback then you will be motivated to try again. I have failed but I am not a failure. The next time I think about failing, I will look to see what I have learned from my failing.

One of the biggest problems that people have with divorce is the drive and desire to move on. I have talked to many people during my years as a pastor. You would be surprised to know how many people stay in or even return to situations that are not healthy and happy because of their inability to simply move on. I have talked to women and men who were afraid because of threats and abuse in their relationships, but they chose to remain in the relationships because they just could not envision MOVING ON.

I remember counseling with a lady who was very unhappy in her marriage. Her husband, in her own words, was treating their dog better than he was treating her. She said to me, "Pastor I have thought about leaving the marriage, but I can't."

I asked her, "Is it that you are afraid to leave because of what he might do to you?"

She said "No! If I left, it would make him the happiest man in the world."

That being said I asked her, "Why then won't you leave?"

She said to me, "Because I love him."

I thought about all of the things that she shared with me concerning his behavior. He would sleep with other women. He was verbally abusive. He would embarrass her in public. He told her that he did not love her; and yet, she said that the reason she would not leave was because she loved him.

I then asked her, "Do you love yourself?"

The problem with people moving on in life is most of the time we love someone else more than we love ourselves. Why is this so? Well, sometimes we need a mate to bring validity to our life. There are many people who do not feel good about themselves unless they have someone in their lives. The sad thing is they will jeopardize everything they have just to keep the relationship. They claim to love their spouses even at their own expense and danger. That should never be!

I believe that when you love someone else more than you do yourself it is because you do not really love yourself. It is then impossible to love someone else until you experience love internally. The queen of soul, Aretha Franklin sang, RESPECT YOURSELF. The message was powerful. An equally powerful message, might I add, is to LOVE YOURSELF. When you love and respect yourself, you will then find the strength to move on regardless of how difficult it might be.

I am afraid that you cannot move on until you LET GO. I like what Paul said to the Philippians:

"I am forgetting those things that are behind and reaching for those things that are before."

You must know when to move on. I am not saying move on when you feel that there is a possibility of reconciliation.

How do you know that there is a possibility of reconciliation or when it is time to move on? The best advice I can share is to consult God. As for me, I fell on my face before God. I would not leave the floor until He spoke to my heart about my situation. I am a living witness that He will speak to you. He will tell you when to move on, when to stay and give you that love for yourself so necessary to be able to also love another.

There is someone out there waiting for you! Remember, to be patient and move at God's timing. There is new mercy for you. I need to share with you the NEW MERCIES that trust in God has afforded me.

Chapter Eleven

NEW MERCIES

I t was the summer of 2007. I had been invited to minister during the National Baptist Convention of America which convened in Orlando, FL. I arrived in Orlando with my daughter and niece on Tuesday morning. My plan was to stay the rest of the week in order that I might sightsee and take them to Disney World. On late Tuesday afternoon, I fulfilled my commitment to preach in a "minister's only" gathering of several hundred ministers from across the nation. It was a cherished and prestigious ministry opportunity. Now I was ready to take my beautiful daughter and lovely niece to the park for the rest of the week, or so I thought.

On Wednesday, I decided to go downstairs to the convention center so that I could attend the afternoon worship. After worship I stood in the hallway in the convention center with one of my fellow colleagues. We were involved in ordinary conversation when, for some reason, out of the corner of my eye, I happened to notice two very attractive young women walking down the corridor. It was an unusual and strange moment in time. I looked at my colleague and nodded in the direction of one of the young women.

"Who is that?" I asked.

He had some knowledge of one of the ladies and asked if she was the one I inquired about. He informed me that she was possibly married already. I assured him that although she was a beautiful lady, it was the other woman who caught my attention. What I had not shared in my initial inquiry was that when I saw this woman, I also heard God speak. He clearly said, "THAT'S YOUR WIFE!"

Don't throw up your hands and say, "Here we go again. This man is a hopeless romantic! He always falls in love at first sight." Please hear me out. I heard **GOD** say, "THAT'S YOUR WIFE!" I did not say that I had fallen in love at first sight. I have since matured and realize that love develops and then grows. I can say that I was overwhelmed by her beauty and even more impressed by her entire demeanor.

She was apparently quite confident. My God, I was drawn! Don't leave me now. It helps to view what God does and how He does things.

The concept of companionship between a man and a woman was first the brainchild of God. Remember, His keen sensitivity and attentiveness to the matter in the Garden of Eden. He saw that Adam would be most complete and a better person with a woman by his side.

Earlier, I promised to be open and transparent. By this time I had been divorced for awhile. I had been estranged even longer. I always knew that one day I would enter into covenant relationship with a woman again, with a wife! Since public disclosure of marital problems and the divorce, I became "ripe picking" for single women interested in getting married. My high profile across the country did not help at all. I found my situation the subject of speculation in an age of high technology. The word spread with rapid transmission around the country. People were sending emails and there was some mention that I might be available on some online blogs. Women were trying to find out the location of my church, my marital status, and the whole nine yards.

When I sang "Jesus, Keep Me near the Cross," I knew that I needed the Lord to keep me – quickly! The merciful gift of a wife, **sent from God**, would help me remain focused and maintain my testimony. Notice I said a wife **sent from God**. So you can only imagine how excited I was when I heard God speak about this mysterious woman being my wife.

The two women in the hallway were both attractive. However, the one who kindled my curiosity was beautiful in a casual, soft, and unique way. I felt sort of like what Michael Jackson said in a song, *"She knocked me off of my feet."* She appeared especially confident and paid me absolutely no attention at all. It was apparent that she definitely wasn't in the hallway in search of a man.

My colleague continued to comment about the chance meeting and the unlikelihood that anything would come of this brief encounter. He considered both women off –limits. STUCK-UP were his actual words. He made it crystal clear that these ladies had already been approached by other eligible bachelors and some ineligible ones as well, but none had any success.

Now, it was my turn to ignore somebody. I paid absolutely no attention to his comments. After all, I only expressed interest in ONE of them. I also did not make a practice of standing in hallways looking for a woman. After he made many remarks that were in opposition to me even approaching her; I looked at him and said, "Be careful what you say because from this point on you are talking about MY WIFE!" In the spirit realm, I had already claimed her as mine.

He laughed at me. That was okay. I knew I heard a voice—THE SUPREME VOICE! I was a praying man and recognized God when I heard Him. I let him have his laugh. I could not blame him. I heard the voice. He didn't.

I tried to catch up to this amazing lady but was detained before I could apprehend her. I just wanted to approach her to see if some kind of dialogue could occur. Oh well, I didn't get to her this time; but I knew that there was another worship service that night, and I would definitely be in attendance and for sure I will speak with her there.

I went to my room and called my best friend to tell him about this "vision of glory" that I just had the privilege to behold. He was excited for me, but I'm sure with some degree of skepticism. We talked for awhile but I then thought about the reason that I had prepared to stay in Orlando the extra days. I had to take my girls to the theme park. How could I take them to the park and be at the service at the same time? I came to the conclusion that my daughter and niece were both teenagers and could do quite well at the park alone. I concluded that maybe they would rather that "old dad" not accompany them.

That evening I took them to the park and gave them instructions not to leave the park for any reason and to call me if they were in need of anything. They were excited and so I then went to church!

I must be honest that this night my real reason for going was not for providential purposes—I was on the prowl in pursuit of my prize. Please don't go "deep" on me now! I am sure that at least some point in your life you have evaluated the best way to capture the eye and heart of another. Maybe you were successful in such efforts and have now been married to that person for many years or just a few. Maybe you lament that you did not handle it properly. Maybe you did nothing about it at all. Well, I had been lonely too long. I had too many meals alone. I had no one to call home to late at night when on the road. Upon my return home, I turned the key to a door that opened to an empty residence. I knew that God had spoken to me concerning this awesomely astonishing and confident lady, and I would not stop short of receiving what God had for me.

Trust God when He speaks and KNOW His voice!

I went to church! Shortly upon my arrival I started to scan the crowd to see if I could identify her location. There she was on the stage in front of the congregation with the other members of the praise team. Little did I know that she could sing. I am now even more intrigued. I didn't know how well she could sing; I didn't care but she was sure good to look at. I watched, with great intrigue, a woman whom God said belonged only to me. I wondered how He was going to "reel her in." Please don't be offended with my sense of humor. It is just a part of my personality. It's the way that God made me. (I'm cracking up with laughter up as I recall this life-changing incident.) Actually, this was a very serious matter.

After the praise team had completed the opening of the service, I watched as they exited through the side door. When they went out I left the service as well. Let me say that singing and leaving was not their usual habit. I discovered that they had been in services since 8:30 that morning. It was also not my normal behavior to go to church and leave before benediction, but I must be honest and you will have to forgive me later. I was in intense pursuit of my WIFE! I never did get to hear the preacher, but I know that God has forgiven me. I approached the guy who sang with them to inquire about her. I found out that her name was Tamara and that she was not married. That's all I needed! All right Doc! I'LL TAKE IT FROM HERE!

I looked around in the hotel lobby to see if I could find her walking around. Then, I saw her. I moved deliberately and debonairly in her direction. She was seated with a group of women from her state convention. It took a lot of courage to approach her among an entire group of women, yet I found myself saying, "May I speak with you for a moment?" She looked startled. She did not know me and had never heard anything about me.

She said, "Who me?"

I said, "Yes you."

The conversation was at best, guarded and a little tense. This young woman had her defenses up with a powerful force. Talking about the whole armor! I introduced myself and engaged in some small talk like: *"Are you enjoying the convention? Where are you from? How do you like Orlando?"* I also asked for her phone number. In return, I received a resounding "NO!"

So much for my confidence!

I must confess that my coolness and debonair demeanor was now shaken. Women will never know how much courage it takes for a man to approach them. I tried to continue the conversation but with very little success. I now saw what my colleague was talking about. I'm not saying that she was stuck-up because she was very cordial but certainly not interested.

I did manage to find out her full name, age and place of residence. That was important to me at the time. I also somehow managed to discover that the following day was her birthday. I asked if I might take her to dinner in celebration while I was still in the city. You guessed it! That seemingly did not appeal to her in any way either. I heard the "NO!" response for the second time. I reluctantly said goodbye and expressed it had been nice meeting her and rushed off—defeated! Finally, she left me in the lobby after a futile attempt to make her acquaintance. I went to my hotel room and prayed. It was personal, very much to the point and without King James' syntax:

"God, what's up? YOU said this is my wife! I am trying to follow YOU! WHY did she act like that? What did I do? What's wrong?"

Please don't be overly concerned with the style of my prayer language. I reverence God! I encourage you to read Psalms and examine some of the moods in which we find David, a man after God's own heart, approaching His heavenly Father. Besides, if you speak with God enough, you will go to Him with familiarity and won't have to use a language or vernacular that does not reflect your true self. After all, prayer should be a conversation—speaking and listening.

After I finished praying, I did listen hoping to hear a word but to my dismay I heard absolutely nothing else from Him at this point. Total silence! God will do you like that sometimes. Finally, I went to sleep and I must say that it was a restless night.

The next morning I woke up early with a bright idea. I guess it came to me in my dreams or did I even sleep. I don't know but I was excited about this new strategy that I was going to use. I remembered that it was her birthday and I had a plan.

The "church grapevine" is a useful, unique, and sometimes valuable commodity. I called a friend who was in attendance at the convention from Houston, Texas and asked if he recognized either of their names. He did not know her very well; however, he knew a little about the friend walking with her in the hallway. I told him I was getting ready to send her some flowers. He told me the friend's full name, and I quickly called the front desk to connect me with their hotel room.

I called the room and this wonderful woman answered. "It's her," I thought and then asked to speak to her friend. I introduced myself and shared that I wanted to send flowers to her roommate, Tamara. She thought that the idea of sending flowers was a nice and appropriate gesture. I inquired about the room number and then extended a pleasant goodbye. I still remember the room number.

That morning, on Tamara's birthday, I sent flowers— wonderful, beautiful roses, and an assortment of other flowers. I remember asking the florist to send her your best arrangement regardless of the cost.

They consented to do that but with one problem. They informed me that the flowers would get there no earlier than two o'clock. I tried to persuade them that it was imperative that they get there before she left the room for the afternoon service. I was pressed for time because it was now Thursday and my flight was scheduled to leave Friday morning. They assured me that they would do their best but two o'clock would probably be the delivery time.

Let's go to plan B! I now needed to go to the noon service but there was a problem. The problem was not my daughter and niece going to the parks; that had already been worked out. The problem was not that I didn't want to go to church again; that was a joy. The problem was in packing for the one day preaching commitment I only brought two suits. I had worn both. I started trying to figure out which one I would wear again because I needed to meet someone and I needed to "dress to impress!" This wasn't lust in operation. Rather, it represented a willingness to finally listen to God's response to my prayers. Remember, during the wedding at Cana, Mary, the mother of Jesus, told the men, *"Whatever the Lord says to do, just do it!"* At this point I was ready to do just what the Lord said. I did not know very much about this lady. All that I knew was that WHATEVER the Lord said, I was going to just do it! I had the faith. If He had a wife for me then I was ready!

I took out the suit that I had preached in on Tuesday knowing that she was not in attendance at the minister's session so it was possible that she didn't see me. Don't ask me if the suit was in the best condition. At that point, I didn't care. I prepared to go to church again hoping to catch a glimpse of "THE PROMISE." Little did I know that the promise seemingly considered me no more than a potential PROBLEM. I did not know why. It was a matter of paradigm, I guess. Anyway, I went to church.

This time the praise team that she was a part of was not ministering instead there was a guest choir. As I entered the convention center, I was escorted to the stage area where many of the officers of the convention sat. Initially, I didn't want to go there but later discovered that it was a blessing in disguise. I was able to see the audience well and saw the very moment that she and her friend entered the service.

She was dressed very well though not flashy but very classy. This was the perfect woman! I guess there are many things that God had to forgive me of because I found myself being disconnected from the service because I was watching her every move. I tried not to stare, but there was like a magnetic pull in operation.

When the choir was singing, I could see her enjoying them and at some points she stood to her feet. When the preacher would hit a powerful point, I could see her applauding in agreement. Just watching her caused me to be hypnotized. I can't say that I didn't enjoy the service because I did. I just enjoyed watching her more.

After the service was over, I vowed within myself to make another attempt to enter into a conversation, which was less guarded and strained—and away from the other women. Like the night before, I sought her out in the crowd after service. My approach was different this time. This was no lady easily picked up or swept off her feet. There are some areas of perception that are keenly sensitized as you assume the role of a pastor. Even though I had yet to really speak with her at length, I could already tell she was well grounded, analytical, strongly opinionated (but not offensively so), and confident in herself. Her inborn radar worked non-stop. She was prepared to arrest a "speeder" or violator. I did not want a citation so I cruised along staying well within the speed limit.

There was an event photographer moving around the facility taking candid shots of attendees. He asked to take the picture of this extraordinary lady and her friend. Of course they declined this opportunity, but I must commend and thank the photographer for his insistence that they allow him to take the photo. I watched Tamara as she moved to the wall where the picture was about to be taken. Her friend, who was still involved in conversation, was a little slow getting to the wall. I thought, "This is my opportunity." I smoothly moved in place next to Tamara and said, "I'LL BE ON THIS PICTURE WITH YOU." Then I looked at the photographer as I slipped my arm around her and said, "Don't we make a cute couple? Take our picture!"

Tamara smiled.

Strategically positioned by God, there was this beautiful older motherly-like woman sitting nearby who said, "Y'all sure do make a cute couple."

God certainly does move in mysterious ways because it was at that point that I knew that I had torn down the Berlin Wall.

I was so thankful for this single bit of affirmation. I could not forget that just yesterday my colleague had laughed at me. He meant no harm. However, I needed someone else to see what I saw in the spirit. It felt good just standing beside her. It also felt good when this wise old woman paid us such a compliment—our first of many. **I don't know who that saintly woman is but whoever you are; God bless you!**

I have that photo to this day sitting on the dresser in our bedroom. It is precious. I look at it every day. It represents the beginning of the manifestation of "THE PROMISE." Although, I would not realize it for some time to come, it was also the beginning of a wonderful relationship. The MAC is BACK!

After the photographer finished, I moved swiftly to try to reintroduce myself. I remember carefully selecting each word. I can hear myself saying slowly, "My name is Clinton McFarland. I am not a murderer, a rapist nor a criminal, and by the way, Happy Birthday!" She replied "Oh, you remembered." I said, "Of course I remembered. Now let me try this again. I simply want to take you to dinner for your birthday and honestly, I will not take no for an answer."

I also later found out that some of the women sitting in the lobby the night before had assessed me as "worthy of further examination" and had shared as much with the woman I longed to know better. These kinds of little female cliques can either open the door for you or SLAM THEM SHUT! Thank you, ladies! You did your part. You helped out a lot. You let God use you. You were right on time! In addition, I am grateful because I was completely out of suits. I had closets full of them at home but not here when I needed them. I now understood the sentiment of many women when they find themselves faced with the "I-have-nothing-to-wear syndrome." It doesn't feel good.

She said YES to my invitation. We settled on a time and decided to go to a Japanese restaurant called Kobe's.

I found Tamara poised and intelligent; a professional and an excellent conversationalist. It was a great evening. After dinner, we returned to the hotel lobby and sat together talking until 4:00 am. The time flew by. I loved every moment! I laughed, enjoyed the conversation immensely and forgot temporarily that I had been so lonely for a long period of time. I asked if I could see her once again early in the morning before I left. We spoke briefly the next day, and I went happily on my way.

I felt as though God was definitely up to something, but it wasn't dancing time yet!

DEAFENING SILENCE!

Remember, at the very end of the Old Testament, God temporarily suspends audible communication between heaven and earth. The ancient prophets delivered no words from Malachi to Matthew, a period of approximately 400 years. Well, I guess I felt like the people who longed for a proceeding word because weeks had gone by, and I had heard nothing from Tamara. This too, felt like 400 years of silence.

She did not return my calls. When I finally conversed with her, it was brief and distant. Her explanation was that she was busy at work and with church activities. After such a wonderful evening and a pleasant goodbye, I heard nothing from her! If she had any interest in me she was doing a remarkable job of not allowing me to sense it. This went on for weeks.

I would rehearse the time that we spent together in Orlando and wonder what changed after we left. Was she playing hard to get thinking that this would make her more desirable? If so, that was unnecessary because she could not be more desirable to me than already.

Was there a significant fellow in Texas that I was unaware of? All I knew was that my attempts to acquaint myself with her were not reciprocated. Honestly, it got to the point where I thought about giving up. After all, she must not know who I am; I thought! I had no problem getting the attention of attractive and eligible women. My ego was now taking over. I felt that I didn't have to run after any woman. But, this one was different.

One Sunday morning, I was really discouraged because of my inability to connect with her. The message seemed not to get through. I surmised that it was probably because she was not aware of the fact that I was really serious. I knew that regrettably men sometimes played games with women in order to get to the "Promised Land." You know what I'm trying to say. I felt that maybe she had her guard up because she feared this. After all, she lived in Texas and I lived in Mississippi, and it was easy for me to say one thing on the phone and have extra activity elsewhere.

So I made one last ditch attempt to assure her that I was serious. I called her before my Sunday service to tell her that I was really serious, and I had strong feelings about her. I wanted a relationship with her and told her so. She was, of course, busy on her way to church and after listening she responded with, "I will get back with you this evening, and we will talk."

I waited all that evening but no phone call. The wait continued.

Monday: No phone call.

Tuesday: No call.

By Wednesday I had come to the conclusion that she was not interested in me and I would just stop calling. In order to force myself not to call, I erased her number from my phone.

Then, maybe two or three days later I received a text message. It was friendly and nice but no mention of our last conversation. There was no, "I've been thinking about you… I miss you…I think of you everyday…I can't wait to see you…I've never met anyone like you…etc." NADA! ZILCH! NOTHING! However, it was enough to put a smile on my face and some hope in my heart. I quickly saved her phone number again with renewed vigor. MAC WAS ENCOURAGED!

After that the conversations became a little more frequent but nothing of any serious nature. They were pleasant and inviting nonetheless. I was appreciative for this minor crack in the wall but wanted more. I knew that she was the one after the NEW MERCY that God had shown me.

OK, by now I was just a little bit pitiful. I was also more than a little bit nervous. My dream was right there, and it had been about a month and a half since I last saw her and it looked like our relationship was no more than an acquaintance. I wanted more. I wanted what God showed me. I wanted to see her and would have quickly caught a plane to Austin, Texas just to take her to dinner. All she had to do was give me a glimmer of hope.

I called a good friend in another state who suggested that if indeed I was really serious that I should make another attempt to speak with her, only this time I should say something even more serious. I thought of something serious to say and called her while she was at work. This really was a no-no because she was always busy and pre-occupied. She had a very demanding job as leader of her team. I wondered if she would answer at all.

She did answer, but I was right again. Maybe it was a self fulfilling prophecy because after answering the phone she told me that she was busy and that she would call me as soon as her task had ended. Honestly, I received that with a tablespoon full of skepticism; but I responded, "OK, I will look forward to talking to you then."

Later that afternoon as I was traveling to my favorite Italian restaurant, I called my friend to tell her of the response that I got from the last call to Tamara. My friend was a woman and maybe she understood women much better than I did. She comforted me with the fact that Tamara would call me. While I was on the phone with my friend, I heard a beep in my phone. I looked at the phone and it was this goddess, Tamara! I quickly told my friend who it was and that I would call her back later. Look out, Jesus!

I answered the phone, and we engaged in some pleasant small talk and then out of the blue I verbalized a more serious thought. I asked, "**Are you going to work all the time when I marry you?** You know that you will be my wife."

I guess that did it! She laughed and responded jokingly, "**NO, I won't! When are you going to marry me**?" From that day to this one, the wall came down. Demolition had occurred. After that we talked everyday and some nights until 2:00 in the morning.

HALLELUJAH!

A good man notices and appreciates a woman who walks godly, displays confidence and does not appear to be desperate!

In this instance, I was the desperate one.

Just like that! Just look at God! I had lost so much sleep since I last saw her at the convention. I could not rest even in the daytime. I found myself just staring off into space wishing the phone would ring. With just a little more faith, I could have laid my head on the pillow over the last few weeks and slept like a baby because God had the matter in the sweet palm of His powerful and all-knowing hand. I wonder if He had been laughing at me again as I grew more and more anxious? I wonder if He thought, "Clinton, my son, I've got this. Don't worry!"

From that day until this one, no matter how frequently or how far I have traveled, Tamara and I haven't missed a day communicating with each other. I found out later that she was initially concerned about a long-distance relationship and potentially being connected with a minister who spent a lot of time traveling. She had heard stories about the kinds of things that can form emotional entrapments and become the source of heartbreak and loneliness in many instances. She wanted no part of this life. She had no desire to be used or abused. She had gone to my ministry website and learned that I was a national evangelist, a man on the move. This fact sent red flags flying!

It became necessary to firstly, win her confidence and secondly, to convince her that God had singled her out as my mate. This was a tall order. She represented new mercy in my life. She became the manifestation of the gift of His grace, forgiveness, tolerance, and provision. This brought me back to a theme I had preached many times: **"If we are willing to SUBMIT, REPENT, and OBEY, things will all line up according to God's redemptive plan."**

I then proceeded to make sure that we became friends and equally sharing partners in relationship. I listened attentively to her and made an effort to survey her emotional needs and aspirations. She did the same for me. Then, I shared my own dream. I was forthright and acknowledged the mandate to serve God for the rest of my life and solicited the support of the woman who could hopefully find it in her heart to commit to the same with equal passion. This time, I knew I could not force my will or dreams on another individual. I had learned my lesson. I told her that I had two of the most wonderful children on earth and that for the rest of my life I would be there for them.

After a pleasant and nearly one year and two month courtship, Tamara became my wife in August 2008. It was a beautiful ceremony that took place at the church where I served as pastor in Columbus, Mississippi. Her family and friends came from Texas and other parts of the country. She forfeited the usual custom of marrying in her home town and in her home church.

A second time I found myself standing at the altar. However, any misgiving or concern that might have been at the back of my mind about our marriage had been addressed and readdressed! I gave Tamara enough time to disclose any opinion, objection, requirement, expectancy, phobia, dislike, preference, agenda or unwillingness. Each of us laid our personalities on the table before one another and allowed the other to take a look. More importantly, we both went before God together and asked Him to take an even deeper look.

Somehow, in that process we made a discovery called compatibility, and we still work on it every day. A much better man stood at the altar on the second time around.

After our wedding, we began a wonderful life together. We spent several blissful days in beautiful Hawaii for our honeymoon. At the time of this writing, we have been together for almost three pleasurable and productive years.

We have since moved to Atlanta, Georgia after I accepted the position of Senior Pastor of the Mt. Pleasant Missionary Baptist Church, one of the great Houses of Worship in the city.

I am so happily married that I have to thank God for Tamara daily. I check my watch or cell phone all day in anticipation of the moment that I will see her. She is by my side in ministry. She is my chief cheerleader and serves as the able President and CEO of the one-member, Clinton McFarland Fan Club! (I am just kidding). I do believe that she loves me, though.

On a serious note, she loves God and worships Him with the same intensity as I. Her eyes moisten at the thought of His goodness and favor upon both of us. Like me, she sheds tears of happiness as she thinks about the many ways He continues to shower blessings on us, our family, and our church. When the weight and pressures of leading a congregation become difficult, she helps me to pray through until God works it out.

She honors and respects my loving and ongoing dedicated relationship with my children. She loves them and treats them as though they are her own because they are a part of me. She has made no attempt to alienate me from them at any time. She has never competed for the attention that belongs rightfully to them. On an ongoing basis, she welcomes them into our home. This is also their home.

As she has ministered to my needs, likewise, I have not neglected her needs for emotional support, her own identity, and true love and affection.

Earlier, I mentioned a lack of mastery of priestly duties. I shared that I did okay in some areas of responsibility and failed miserably at others. I want to continue to operate in a spirit of humility; however, I will share that Mrs. Tamara McFarland longs for nothing. Absolutely NOTHING! The priest of our home has finally gotten the hang of things.

Are we rich? Hardly! However, EVERYTHING that she needs within a marriage and in a husband is at her FULL disposal. If something is going on in life that troubles her, it does not matter if I am out of town or at the church; all she has to do is to share her concern with me, and I will either get to her or bring her to me – QUICKLY! Remember, I needed something "serious" to say to her quickly as I first met her. At the time, I needed to maintain her attention. According to the old folk, "Whatever it takes to GET an individual is also what it takes to KEEP them." Tamara gets a "QUICK" and attentive response from me. She too, does a marvelous job of responding to my call.

She makes me laugh. She tolerates my human frailty and shortcomings. She is sensitive even to my irritability. She knows when I "need my space." She lovingly oversees my eating habits and expertly and efficiently maintains our home. She understands my responsibility, even those financial aspects to my children and my former wife. And yes, like any godly Proverbs 31 woman, she keeps me in reasonable check. It is a part of her assignment. As I shared earlier, a woman's role involves being the HEART of her house. She certainly is my heart! God gave her to me, and I daily thank Him for NEW MERCIES.

Chapter Twelve

BEFORE YOU LEAP

There are many of you who are either seeking to remarry or contemplating marriage for the first time. Before entering marriage, I encourage you to explore every avenue through which a door may be opened that could lead to serious challenges. As a pastor and counselor, I have found that certain scenarios tend to repeat themselves. It is imperative that you know what I learned the hard way. Although I am adjusting, I will have to deal with certain situations for the rest of my life.

We certainly are human and unfortunately, we have the capacity, propensity, and proclivity to mess up. It's inevitable. It is a part of our Adamic nature. Even when I endeavor to do right, I end up doing wrong. The Apostle Paul realized this in the passage where he said, *"That which I should do, I do not and that which I should not do, I do.*" The fact of the matter is that as long as we are in the world we will experience some degree of messing up. It's sort of like that popular rap group from the 90's. We are just "NAUGHTY BY NATURE."

I'm not passing out licenses to mess up because there are certainly consequences for our failures; but the fact is, we, at some point, will mess up in some way or another. While I feel no obligation to divulge any additional "mess ups" in my former marriage, I will say that there were more. Some of which I'm embarrassed to divulge in full details. There were some things I committed and some other things I omitted. One can be as damaging as the other.

There are certain things that should take place in a marriage and when these things are omitted, your marriage can be in just as much danger as when there are committed mess-ups. There were examples of both in my former marriage. Had we known better, we possibly would have done better. I don't want this to happen to you so read carefully!

My father used to speak about a thing called the sin of omission and the sin of commission. His explanation was simplistic:

Commission is when you are actively involved in a sin.
Omission is when you are inactive in what is right.
Commission is when you succeed in doing wrong.
Omission is when you fail in doing right.

In most instances, people certainly don't start out in marriage with the intention of messing up but somewhere down the road complacency, coupled with selfishness, creeps in and they start taking the marriage for granted. This opens the door for "mess ups" to invade the relationship. The mess-ups that result are varied in nature.

The Mess-Up of Omission

Let's start with those things that couples omit doing. These are things that you should consider before you leap.

I've discovered that the greatest way to mess up is probably not in what you do, but in what you fail to do.

Omission #1: Verbalizing Love...

When you omit sharing the fact that you love your spouse, you then take it for granted that they already know. I have heard it said time and time again: "You know that I love you because I pay the bills; don't I?" The man would say this as if his wife is the only one benefiting from bills being paid. You pay the bills because you like the lights on. You pay the bills because you like your house cool in the summer and warm in the winter. When you love someone you should not omit saying it or showing it in special ways.

Also in counseling I have repeatedly heard, "You know that I love you because I cook, clean, and take care of your children." The woman would say this as if cooking and cleaning only benefited her husband. Of course we know that the children are not his only. If you love someone then it should be verbalized and not expected to be something that is understood or assumed. Many couples are guilty of this omission. I trust you realize the power of spoken words and the spiritual implications of this powerful con-fession. What if every married couple found that at least once each day they uttered the words "I LOVE YOU" to their spouse? Your spouse may know it but still they need to HEAR IT!

Omission # 2: Sharing in Obligations...

When you experience this omission it can leave your spouse feeling more like a servant than a spouse. We cannot leave the entire child-raising responsibilities to one spouse. We cannot leave the burden of nurturing the relationship to the other person. It is crucial that we share in the obligations of the marriage. When we fail to share in assuming responsibility, we mess-up through omission. It is said that for a marriage to work, both persons must willingly contribute at least fifty percent. That sounds good in theory; however, I believe that the contribution should be one hundred percent from each person. I am aware that it's not possible to give one hundred percent all the time but that should be the goal. Two hundred percent is hard to beat!

I am always amazed when I talk with couples who have been married for fifty years plus. I discover much wisdom in the area of marriage. Many experts can write a book on marriage but these couples have lived the book!

One couple told me that the important key to their fifty plus year marriage was the understanding that there are times when the other person has to give more. They said that sometimes the husband is not doing all that he should do so the wife has to pull the greater load. Sometimes the wife is not doing all that she should do so the husband has to pull the greater load. It is not always fifty-fifty. Sometimes it is seventy-thirty or sixty-forty, but in order to make the marriage work you have to be willing to push or pull as much as necessary. It is called SHARING IN OBLIGATIONS.

Omission # 3: Sharing in Prayer...

As a Christian, I believe in the power of prayer. I also believe that prayer is essential for one's life to be made whole. Since this is so for the individual, then it stands to reason that it is also true for the married couple. The Bible says that *"for this cause shall a man leave his father and mother and cleave unto his own wife and they shall be no longer twain but one flesh."* According to Scripture, when a man and woman choose to unite in holy matrimony, they are no longer two separate entities operating but they become one flesh. They operate as one person. It is important to build a solid front fortified with prayer.

Many successful couples do this from the beginning. They take time to pray and affirm their prayers and petitions through the Scripture. This is something that I would see my father do for our family. We would listen to sermons and lectures concerning marriage, family building, and other important matters. This is why, in spite of our naiveté in the beginning, marriage works. We see manifestation of the answers to our prayers. The Lord increases our blessings and as a result we became busier. It continues to the point that we become too busy to take time to pray and read our Bible together. We are so consumed in reaping the harvest that we neglect to plant new seeds or make new deposits of joint prayer. There is a lesson to be learned here. If there is no spiritual relationship in the home, there is no dynamic relationship in the marriage. As our joint prayer life diminishes, (representing the lifeblood of godly relationship) our marriage has little with which to sustain itself. You are then headed toward cardiac arrest.

Omission # 4: Unwillingness to continue learning and growing...

Many times we learn about marriage from watching our parents or some other influence in our life. When we make the decision to marry most of us understand the need for some pre-marital counseling. After we are married, some of us even read a book or take advantage of an available marriage seminar. All of that is good and recommended. The problem is that after some years, one or maybe both persons may feel that this is no longer needed. We think that because we are doing well we've perfected our roles. That's a huge mistake and a subtle trick of the enemy.

I now believe that marriage is a constant work in progress. Regardless of the length of your marriage, you have never fully apprehended. You will never get to the point where you have arrived. There must be a constant pursuit of progress. So, what I am saying is that what we do in the beginning with good results, we must continue all the way through.

In our churches, we must provide the opportunity for married couples to rekindle or refresh their relationships. At least once a year there should be some kind of marriage seminar given for married couples. Seminars are necessary because they introduce us to new ideas and cause us to see some things about ourselves that our spouse may not be able to articulate.

There also must be a constant flow of good marital teaching and principles in the home. Regardless of how long you have been married, there are still some areas in which you can improve. There is too much information available to allow the growth of a relationship to become stagnant. The Internet is a powerful communication and teaching tool. It is a major resource and can be used to find Christian literature as well as radio/television programming concerning marriage. It is imperative that we continue to learn. It always amazes me how we are very interested in learning in order to receive promotions on our jobs. We will go to college for years and then participate in continuing education after we graduate in order to advance occupationally. Well that same interest and pursuit is necessary if we are to have long lasting marriages.

Omission # 5: Perpetuating the Passion...

When couples are first married there is a certain passion that they enjoy. Usually it grew and developed as a result of the dating process. It is astonishing that when they are dating they can't see enough of each other. They love spending time together. They call and talk for hours at a time. I remember one couple sharing with me about their dating experiences and how when they were dating they hated hanging up the phone. They would have little debates about who should hang up first: *You hang up first; no you hang up; no you hang up first; well let's hang up together. Let's hang up on the count of three; one, two, three, click.* They would give little gifts that say I love you and I'm thinking about you. He enjoyed opening the door for her and being considerate of each other's feelings. All of this contributed to building passion. It continued for a while after they were married but somewhere down the path something happened. Let's examine the cause.

For most people, marriage is an end goal and not a developing process. For some, marriage has become something to APPREHEND but not to MAINTAIN. The ultimate goal is to find the right person and get married.

You are in love and happy but because of your naivety you feel that this is all it takes. After a while the phone calls are shortened, the gifts cease, the car door is no longer opened, and the special acts of kindness disappear. Before you know it, the passion that you once enjoyed has died. What did Mr. B. B. King say? **"The thrill is gone."**

This, of course is not something that we do on purpose yet, it happens. It happens because we become so enamored with other important things like children, careers, budgets, and accommodations. These are important things but not the most important thing. The most important thing should be to take care of your spouse.

When we omit, we're just as much to blame as the one who commits. I can say this, because while we can confess to aspects of commission, we are at greater fault in omission. On the other side of a marital storm, I have some advice for pastors and busy men as you continue to enter dates in your blackberry—the almighty tool which takes us from month to month, from one municipality to another, from one coast to the other, from frigid climates to the tropics, from takeoff to landing. Please know that I preach first to myself so that I will not repeat some of the misgivings below. Please consider the following and avoid a waiting disaster:

- Don't forget to schedule some time to go home and immediately pull the love of your life into your arms.
- Don't forget to schedule enough time to just hold her and listen to what she might be going through.
- Don't forget to allow enough time to listen to what might be going on in the lives of your children—even if you have just returned home from a demanding and grueling responsibility.
- Don't neglect to schedule the time to hear what God might be speaking to her.
- Don't forget to take the time to regularly schedule a "date" for the two of you. During this time, please make time to completely mesmerize her with **genuine** words of **affection** and **appreciation.**
- Don't forget, PASTORS, as you go out on the next crusade to win the world that the first Christian battlefront remains maintaining your relationship and home. Don't forget that she and your family are at home, waiting and depending upon you. Find time

not to disappoint them. While you are away and possibly a little stressed trying to manage a church over the phone, text messaging, or through email, remember she might have equal challenges caring for the family and household without you.

- Don't forget to schedule time to pray just for her. After all, next to Jesus, she is probably your most effective, dedicated, and most well-meaning intercessor.
- Don't forget to schedule vacations and getaways where you are just her husband and the children's father.
- Don't forget to schedule other overnight getaways when you are just HERS—no children, no business partners, no secretaries, no government officials, and no interviews.

If you wish to be treated like a king, then by all means I suggest that you make sure that the queen at home has your attention.

More than "things" she really needs YOU! Nothing else will compensate—not cars, fine homes, furs, clothes, prestige, or a specially designated seat in the sanctuary.

God did not substitute material possessions as prerequisites for happiness in the garden. He DID strongly allude to COMPANIONSHIP. He made HER for YOU and likewise, He made YOU for HER! Please listen to the voice of experience. I have suffered through this storm.

I also have some advice for spouses of pastors and busy men: As all of the above behaviors prayerfully come into manifestation, receive it with **grace, sweetness, and appreciation**. Just tell God, "Thank You" for any small signs of improvement or extra attention. Also, make it known to your spouse that you appreciate their efforts in serving God and in ministering personally to you.

Somewhere, along the way, we become so involved that one agenda takes unfair precedence over another. Too often, it is the home and family relationship that pays the price. It is up to BOTH OF YOU TO KEEP THE SHIP AFLOAT!

Right now I feel like contacting all of the marriage counselors in the country who counsel spouses whose marriages are in trouble. I feel like suggesting that they take down their shingles, web pages, and blogs because from my own experience, coupled with the experiences of other clergy, I have now publicly and spiritually addressed the answers to many of the basic problems in many of our homes. And, I did not charge a fortune!

What qualifies me to offer suggestions and such antidotes? The sad truth is that after a period of time, having no idea how to proceed with needed sensitivity and preserve a relationship with my ex-wife, I was forced to forfeit my dream of providing the same kind of stable home environment that my father created for me and my siblings. I failed to accomplish, on a consistent basis, some of what I just suggested for you. It's a hard thing to admit but it's true. I share this because there are countless repeat versions of this saga in the lives of many men today.

I hope my story will help you to keep your relationship whole. In your role as a man, I pray you will reassess a more significant role in terms of your wife and family. In the midst of all we are called upon to do, it takes work to keep all of this in proper perspective. I salute you for all that you do. The ongoing responsibility upon us is monumental.

You would not want to go through what I have experienced. It was not pretty. There were times when I felt as though I would lose my mind; but thank God that I made it, and I'm ALL RIGHT NOW!

I also have some basic observations for individuals who have never been married or who are considering another marriage. This thing called pre-marital counseling can define and shape the dynamics of true happiness. Given today's statistics, I am unwilling to perform a marriage ceremony if extensive counseling has not taken place.

The Bible speaks of being "unequally yoked." Sometimes we march down the aisle knowing that there are major problems; however, we are caught up in the moment, bedazzled by the lovely woman in a wedding gown, the handsome man at the altar, the limousine and the waiting honeymoon. Sometimes, we rush to that same altar because we feel no one else will come along. Sometimes, too many of our friends have entered into marriage, and we feel left out. Sometimes someone has convinced us that the Lord has spoken and that we belong to them. Sometimes, as Christians, we want to be free to engage in the sexual privileges of a marriage relationship without condemnation.

The Power of Connection

Unfortunately, for every other person who entered into marriage, there was no fail-proof manual of instructions available for our use. Consequently, we were forced to just sort of feel our way along through trial and error. The errors are so numerous, at times, that the relationship is finally destroyed.

The age-old definition of insanity admonishes us not to do the same thing over and over again if we expect different results. As I have shared, I am now married to a wonderful woman whom GOD sent to me. As I entered the marriage relationship a second time, I wanted to make sure that I did not commit those errors which helped to weaken my first relationship. **One wise person said that wisdom does not come from experiences but what we do with experiences.** I reluctantly revisited the man in the mirror and took a good look at who I had been, what I had done, who I had become and how I could avoid the unpleasant occurrence of divorce. There are certain things that I make a conscious effort to accomplish. These are a few of the connecting behaviors that I have adopted. Before you take the leap or if you have already leaped, please consider this behavior...

1. I am not sure that it is possible for one human to be responsible for another's happiness; however, **I resolved to personally make sure that I helped my wife to be able to be happy.** It is true that no one person can actually make another person happy; however, we can make a happy person unhappy. We can also help a happy person to remain happy. Therefore, I worked on making a happy woman even happier.

2. I committed to **"STUDY"** the marriage relationship by reading books, visiting marriage-enhancing web-sites, listening to available CD series and attending seminars. I invited my wife to be an active partici-pant and contributor to this process. We found that books bring things to the surface that we may have not have considered or did not volunteer to share initially.

3. **I accepted the fact that men and women are dif-ferent emotionally**. I work to understand and be

sensitive to these differences. After determining general differences between men and women, it is necessary to study "MY" woman. She is an individual and a unique creature made by God.

4. I made a deliberate **effort to discuss** points of disagreement or concerns ONLY when we were engaged in regular conversation and not during arguments.

5. I make sure that my wife understands how much **I appreciate her willingness to take an active role as my mate** and the First Lady of a growing congregation. She is not only my marriage partner but she is my "balance." In many instances, she is the voice of my "conscience."

6. Rather than taking the good and special things that she does for granted, **I have adopted a regular practice of positive reinforcement.** For example, she wonderfully maintains her personal appearance and keeps a pristine house. She oversees my diet and makes sure that I have not only the food that I enjoy but the foods that are healthy. I REWARD her by saying, "thank you," "you look really good," "the

house looks great" and "thanks for controlling your spending!" (smile). It works; a happy wife makes a happy home. A smart and considerate husband will build upon this happiness. I also show up with flowers and trinkets to accent my appreciation.

7. **I have invited her into my world** as well as worked to make it a pleasant world in which to dwell. She accompanies me on evangelistic endeavors and oversees that leg of my ministry responsibilities.

8. **I LISTEN** with great care to what she has to say. She has a well-earned right and a privilege of sharing an opinion.

I know now that it appears that men and women are on a different page. Not only are there physiological differences but just as important, there are emotional differences. We are different in our ideology and in our attitude. This difference in attitude can certainly lead to a world of conflict and misunderstanding. For example, some studies suggest that the average woman utters 25,000 words on a given day. In contrast, the average man is credited with approximately 5,000 words. For some, this would suggest that women are talkers and men are thinkers. Actually, a better or perhaps "more safe" assessment might be that women and men process and deal with situations differently. More specifically, when there is a problem in the house with the family or relationship, women would rather talk it out. In many instances, a man would rather think it out and postpone discussion. This can be a source of great frustration for the woman, who by her very nature, NEEDS to talk! The man by contrasting nature NEEDS her to give him some space and the privilege of being quiet until he is ready to talk. He may pull away and become silent for a period of time, but the wife is filled with an unfulfilled emotional need to get things out for discussion.

How do we address these differences? How do we ensure a reasonable "connect" with the person we love? Proverbs 4:7 says, *"Wisdom is the principal thing; therefore get wisdom: and with all thy getting get understanding."* So I must understand the need for me to talk and listen to my wife. I am wise enough to know that her emotional needs require that someone will take the time to listen. If I am not the receptacle of her inner thoughts, then someone else will be. Sadly, this is how a lot of affairs begin.

We must become better communicators. I have dis-covered that communication in a marriage is paramount. I have to own up to the fact that men are not known as the best communicators. In all my years of being a pastor and counseling, very few women have told me that their husbands are good communicators. Rather, they have told me that their husbands are not good listeners. They find it very difficult to maintain their undivided attention. They also need men to listen more than they need them to work it out or tell them what to do.

The next thing that will help us connect with our spouse is when we are secure enough to be vulnerable. What do I mean by this? Most men think that women want or are impressed by men who are made of stone. My counseling experience bears another story. From my vantage point and experience, women want men to share their personal experience, their fears, hurts, AND, their emotions.

In all likelihood, if a woman is hurting, afraid, con-fused or in pain she will have no problem in letting you know. Men, on the other hand will camouflage even small emotions in order to maintain a certain "image." Remember, when we were little boys our fathers would tell us to be tough and be a man. In contrast, little girls would hurt themselves and Mommy and Daddy bathed them with kisses and comfort. Sometimes, they would cry with them. This imprinting has become a part of the male psyche. Too often we have been conditioned to be silent, wear emotional masks, and pretend that certain things just don't exist.

Finally, men and women are different when it comes to intimacy. Women are stimulated mostly by touch, but not necessarily in the private areas of their bodies. They like ongoing affection and nice things said to them. Again, in contrast, men are stimulated by sight. Making allowances for these differences we end up with these kinds of scenarios:

- Women enjoy and want a man who is romantic! One wife told me that she wanted to be treated the same as when they were dating. She wanted to be called from work even when he wanted nothing in particular. She wanted him to hold her hand. She wanted gifts— just because, not because it was her birthday or their anniversary. I have some special advice for the men:

You will experience a lot more good nights if you romance your wife every chance you get. These are the kinds of things that are romantic to a woman.

* With men, romance usually involves getting to the "Promised Land" as quickly as possible. Additionally, men do like feeling like a king whether it's in bed or out.

Mind you, I am not about to give the impression that all women or men are exactly alike however, there are many similar traits found within most. I would encourage each of you, husbands and wives, to study YOUR SPOUSE as though you are trying to make the honor roll or the coveted "Dean's List." When you have worked diligently on your relationship with such intensity, you will be much closer in the discovery of the power of connection with your spouse.

Commission...

I will not spend time on the committed mess-ups because we are usually pretty conscious of them. For example, infidelity, lying, abuse, verbal abuse, and betrayal can be deadly to any marriage. I hope that every person who is reading this book is mindful of this already. For some of us even though we are conscious of how destructive these things can be to a marriage, we find ourselves engaging in these sins. Might I suggest something for those who have yet to take this leap – consider staying single until you are ready to <u>not</u> commit either of those non-erasable sins. For instance, if you have a problem with infidelity it will not change just because you get married. Lying, abuse, verbal abuse, and betrayal will certainly cause your marriage to come to an end.

These are committed mess-ups that will destroy the strongest marriage and even if you have much love for your spouse it will not be strong enough to keep you together.

Other Counter-Productive Forces...

There are other counter-productive forces that I want you to consider before you take the leap or jump the broom. Many of these I know about from personal experience.

◊ Marrying too Young

Marrying too young is certainly a factor, which contributes significantly to the dissolution of many marriages. When you are a child you have yet to learn certain things about yourself. This makes it difficult to get to know someone else.

Many people who marry young feel that they know what they are doing. After all, you are in love, but several years later you will discover that there are so many areas in your personality that should have been developed prior to marriage. I genuinely believe that before two become one, there must be individual wholeness. Simply stated, **you must be whole alone before you can be whole together.**

I had one couple to share with me that from the beginning, they were not complete. They were still children. They had not given themselves time to become complete or mature. The process of becoming whole takes time. When you are not whole alone, it is then that you look for the person closest to you to validate you or make you whole. What an unfair burden! I must pause to issue an alert to those of you who are contemplating marriage. **Don't get married until you are a whole person all by**

yourself. Otherwise, you will place a tremendous burden on the other person in the relationship.

I know that there are some couples who married young and have been married for fifty years, but I guarantee you that if they were honest they would tell you not to do the same thing. I believe they would tell you to take your time, secure a career, and devote time to self-development. They would tell you this because of difficulties in their marriage, particularly in the early years. The only reason why they are still together is because they made the decision to stick with it no matter what. I must applaud them for cleaving to each other and sticking to their vows.

There was another couple who shared with me that they were having problems in their marriage and years passed by before they were able to recognize what was going on. All they knew was that something was wrong and the marriage was not working. After talking with them and hearing both sides, I asked them to describe each other. After their descriptions, I then asked them to share what it was that they liked about each other that made them fall in love. After listening to their descriptions of each other and their other feelings, I was able to discover the problem. I shared with them that the person whom you married is not the person whom you are with now. The problem with marrying young is that what you get at eighteen or nineteen is not what you wake up to at thirty-five or thirty-six. People develop, they evolve and what they become may not fit your maturing personality. This development or evolution is inescapable.

I have asked many people privately this question, "Would the person who you are with be the person whom you would marry if you were marrying today?" Sadly, for many the answer was a resounding no. The reality is that there are many tell-tale signs that occur in a relationship prior to the pronouncement of the nuptials. Many of these signs are ignored and disregarded, but there was good news in this question that I raised.

There were others who in evaluation of their spouses have shared that faced with marriage again they would do it the same way and with the same person. What a wonderful declaration!

The fact that there are so many who would not do it the same way does not speak to the fact that their spouse is unsuitable, but it speaks to the fact that there were some obvious incompatibilities in the relationship. You can raise children together, buy a house together, and even display a wonderful public front and still not be compatible. You can even love each other but have personalities that are too conflicting. Many couples who divorce make much better friends than they do spouses. Marrying too young will contribute much to the late discovery of this incompatibility, which will hide itself during the courtship and early years together.

I must reaffirm the fact that I don't claim to be an expert on this subject matter but because of a failed marriage and the privilege that I have to talk to so many couples, I can see things more clearly. I'm a great believer in the sanctity of this godly union, but I also feel that it is incumbent upon us to do certain things in order for us to not repeat past failures, foolishness, and fallacies. Once this has occurred it is then that you are on your way to a happy and healthy future.

CHAPTER 13

RISE AND BE HEALED!

Perhaps you are in the process of divorce or you have been divorced for a while? You may wonder if there is any way that healing is possible after going through such emotional affliction and turmoil. I would like to be a part of the discovery of that answer for you. And, my answer is— YOU BET! IT IS VERY POSSIBLE TO HEAL FROM DIVORCE! Total healing is a part of my personal testimony. Not only is it possible, but in order for you to live a fulfilled life, it must occur. It is a necessity!

I believe that the general consensus among most people is that they want to be whole; they want to experience happiness, and they want to enjoy life. In order for these things to occur, healing from an emotionally trying event must take place. There are those who erroneously believe that because the papers have been signed that this dismal chapter in their life is finally over. Nothing could be further from the truth! It is a fallacy of mega proportions; yet, many people fall into this category. Actually, for a moment, I thought so as well.

I remember saying that if I could just get this part of my life over (speaking in reference to the divorce procedures) I could then move on. Lord, was I wrong! The only thing that was over was the legal process. The legality of our being apart had been addressed – the dividing of the assets and arrangements which involved the children, but there is something about marriage that inevitably leaves an attachment. Anytime you are in a relationship with someone there is something that you leave with them and something that they leave with you. This residue or attachment is powerful and unavoidable.

It's kind of like the little boy whose friends dared him to kiss the side of the house in sub-zero weather. He soon discovered something very significant and equally painful about attachment. After he finally pulled himself from the house, he discovered that a portion of him was left on the house and a portion of the house was left on him.

The process of ending a marriage is similar. Regardless to how difficult the marriage may have been, you may have wanted the divorce or it may have been the idea of your spouse, the residue of attachment was inevitable—probably for both of you. Just as the little boy with injured lips needed care and healing, you too will need to go through a healing process.

The Bible teaches that when a man and woman choose to unite in holy matrimony, the man will leave mother and father and cleave unto his wife. You may ask, exactly what does this mean? It means that a man will restructure his relationship and allegiance with his mother, father, and all other relationships and will become more permanently and intimately attached to his wife. In other words, it does not mean that a man will no longer recognize or respect his parents, but that relationship will not take precedence over the covenant relationship that he has with his wife.

In marriage, your wife biblically becomes the closest person to you. She becomes an extension of your very being. So you have formed a union with a human being. You have granted access to the most sensitive part of your heart and soul. The act of divorce severs this strong connection; and it HURTS!

When something involves process, it indicates that it takes time to be complete. You should not expect, as I did, that healing will be complete overnight. We would love to experience healing with one dose of prayer or one session of reading a Scripture; but that's not going to happen in this case. The healing process must be allowed to run the prescribed course.

When I was a boy of about seven or eight years old, I remember playing on the side of the bed. Because of the positioning of the bed there was very little room between the bed and the wall. I was jumping and playing not knowing that there was a cross-cut-saw stored between the bed and the wall. I guess I jumped one time too many and cut a piece of skin from my leg. My mother immediately applied medicine to the cut and placed a bandage on it. The antibiotic protected it from germs and harmful bacteria. The bandage provided a protective covering. Underneath the bandage a healing process began. The bandage and the medicine worked together.

This childhood incident taught me a lot about the healing process. I would have loved for healing to have occurred immediately because with healing the unbearable pain would have come to an end. Sometimes the healing process can be accelerated with the proper application of the right medicine. In contrast, the process can be interfered with or prolonged and will cause infection to occur. My mother covered the open wound with a bandage which accomplished two things. First of all, it kept it from view decreasing the likelihood that I would open it again. Next, it protected the area from dirt and harmful bacteria that could impede the healing process.

Because the proper process took place, the deep cut has totally healed. But then there is a scar that serves as a constant reminder of what happened. Some thirty-five years later that scar still remains but it doesn't hurt anymore. In actuality, I thank God for the scar because it reminds me to be a little more PATIENT and CAREFUL and to **be careful where I jump.**

Slowing the Healing Process

The healing process is already slow enough, but sadly there are those who go through divorce unaware of certain inevitable factors and end up slowing the process of healing. You don't do this on purpose, but when you don't know how to allow your emotions to heal; then you can and will unintentionally slow down the process.

How do we slow down the process? One of the main things that we unintentionally do is to deny the need to heal. We don't want to deal with it. We think that the situation will just go away. Whenever you don't deal with a situation, it will deal with you. Many people have experienced mental problems and nervous breakdowns because they chose to ignore the problem. The breaking of a marriage is like an emotional cut. If my mother had not known what to do when my leg was cut, then it would have healed much slower or may not have healed at all.

Speeding the Healing Process

Of course we know that all people do not heal at the same pace. Thank God for that! I also thank God that I chose to heal at a more rapid pace because firstly; I finally realized that I needed to heal and secondly; as a pastor and experienced counselor, I had some idea of what it was that I needed to do to get on track.

One of the reasons why I believe that the Lord inspired me to write about divorce is to help millions of people who are going through divorce to heal properly. Since I don't know the extent of your attachment, I cannot begin to forecast how long healing will take; but I do know that God, in His grace, has built within us the emotional capacity to heal. Our actions and attitude can ACCELERATE the process or IMPEDE it.

The following are some of the things which I elected to do to get through the process:

- **I finally faced my hurt and pain head on**. I stopped trying to act like I was alright when I was about to die inside. Honestly, that's how I felt when I was going through my divorce and the healing process. Many people didn't know it because I was careful whom I exposed my hurt to because it would have given some people too much joy to see me so devastated.

- **I did not lie to myself.** Even though I did not fully divulge my hurt to my parishioners; in the secret of my mind, I did tell MYSELF the truth. You will slow the healing process when you refuse to be truthful with yourself. You may play a fair game of deception with others but ultimately this same deception doesn't work as well on you. If you are hurting then admit you are hurting. If you are angry then admit you are angry. I'm not of the opinion that you can ignore your problems or deny the existence of circumstances and expect that everything will be all right.

  Jesus walked up to the man who was laid at the pool of Bethesda and said, *"Will thou be made whole?"* If the man had said, "I'm already whole; I know they say I'm sick but I don't claim it," he would have never been healed. Consequently, I told myself the truth about how I felt.

- **I went deep into prayer.** Let me add that when I prayed not only did I tell myself the truth, I told God the truth. The best thing that you can do when you pray is to tell God how you really feel. When I read the Psalms I am encouraged to know how honest the psalmists were with God. When they were hurting they told Him. When they were mad, even if it was with God, they still told Him. We should never be afraid to tell God how we really feel. The fact of the matter is that He already knows. You may be thinking, since He knows already then why should I tell him? You should tell Him for two reasons. Firstly; this exchange is therapeutic. Secondly; He expects us to present our challenges to Him. That's why He's known as GOD! I went deeply into prayer; I developed a prayer life like never before. I have always prayed because I believe so strongly in prayer but never like I did during this time of special struggle.

What is prayer? Prayer is a dialogue and not the monologue we often carry to God. A monologue is when only one does the talking. A dialogue is when two are involved. As I mentioned above, there is an exchange in place. This is significant because we must realize that when we talk with God it is vital that WE ALLOW HIM to talk with us. That's the consummation of prayer. When we finish talking, we must stay in a position where we then hear from God.

Through this ordeal, I developed a real friendship with God. I found a place where I felt so much closer to God. I have always felt closer to God out in nature. I don't know why this is so; maybe because I have the privilege to observe God's natural creations. I look at the trees and flowers. I look at the sky and the little rivers and streams. All of these were created by God. There is a nature trail in the town of Columbus, Mississippi, where I once lived, called the "River Walk." It goes down through the woods and runs sometimes parallel with the river. That was the place that I met with God most often. It was there that I would go without a pager, cell phone, or mp3 player and just open up to God. It was there that I could be totally honest with Him. It was there that I could hear Him speak to me most clearly. You would be surprised to know some of the things that we talked about. These moments were precious and intimate. It remains between God and me. It made a better person out of me. It accelerated my healing.

- **I Exercised! Exercised! Exercised!** What does physical activity and exercise have to do with one healing from the breakup of a marriage? Well, we all know that with any turbulent and trying situation, inescapably there is stress and anxiety. I remember being so stressed as a result of this difficult process. Stress can cause physical problems and anatomical ailments. Many people develop ulcers and other stomach problems as a result of a stressful situation. Here I was going through a divorce, pastor of a growing and demanding church, preaching in over forty different cities over the course of a year, trying to comfort my children, and dealing with a ton of rumors all at the same time. You talk about pressure, anxiety, and stress, I had them! Some days my body would be in so much pain until I felt like I was having a nervous breakdown. I discovered that the more I exercised the less stress I felt. When you are going through the healing process it does not do you any good to breakdown under pressure or develop some other physical problems. I advise you to get into a good exercise program. This will certainly help the healing process.

- **Talk! Talk! Talk!** Most of us who go through a divorce really need therapy. Many people can't afford it and some of us can't seem to find the time. Therapy gives us an opportunity to vent some of our frustrations. In other words, **we need to talk it out.** Those of us who have been to a therapist have discovered that the therapist does very little talking. It is because he or she knows that the answer to your problem lies within you; and if they allow you to do the talking, the solution will come more quickly. So they get paid a hundred dollars per hour or more just to listen to you rant and rave and then they just analyze what you said, put it into perspective, and remind you of what YOU said YOU need to do. Talking is therapeutic. At first when I was going through the worst part of my breakup, I found myself talking to everyone whom I could about my situation. In retrospect, that was not the smartest thing to do. I made regrettable mistakes in sharing with certain people. Even though I made mistakes, it was something that I couldn't seem to help. I had so much hurt pinned up inside of me until I felt like I would burst if I couldn't get it out. I want to warn you to be smarter than I was, but by all means "Talk, Talk, Talk." GET IT OUT! Every time you strategically "talk out" your problems you are a step closer to healing.

It is also important that you talk to people who are not so quick to give you their opinions. That can be more confusing than helpful. In fact, I found myself not wanting others' opinions. I gravitated to the people who would just provide an ear and lend support. I encourage you to be selective with whom you talk to. Good can come from such sharing. Indiscriminate selection of confidants can also complicate your problems.

Still in Love

You would be surprised to know how many people stand before a judge and declare the need to sever their marital ties and they are still in love. They still think about their spouse all the time. A matter of paper and pen does not mean it's over. I call the pen and paper, the "commencement" and the "consummation" of the divorce.

There are many who are holding out hope that one day they will be together again. I know because this is something that I went through. I would make subtle advances and try being extra nice and kind. I would call more than was necessary to check on the children. Every time, the advances were seemingly ignored. It was like being rejected all over again. My acts of kindness would go unnoticed, like coming over to fix something or other matters. They all brought few results. It was disheartening. I would call and either there was no answer or she was already on the phone in conversation.

I was divorced and occasionally dating someone else and still very much in love with my ex-wife. I share this because this is the way I felt – still in love but no reciprocity from the one who happened to be the object of my affection. Still in love, but what do you do about being in love with someone who has chosen not to make your house a home?

I DON'T WANT YOU TO BE CONFUSED! This is certainly in the PAST and is not applicable to my life now.

But I do understand that some of you reading this book can certainly relate to what I felt at THAT time.

We had been together for seventeen years, sixteen years of marriage plus one year of dating. I wondered if it was going to take another seventeen years before I no longer had these feelings. It would have been nice if I could have just turned my emotions off, but the fact of the matter is that love is so powerful until it causes you to ignore so many things, so many hurts, so many pains and you find yourself loving even when there's no reciprocity in place. So what do you do?

Accept the Inevitable

What do I mean by inevitable? There are some things in life we must learn to accept. We have no control over them. When a person chooses to discontinue or sever the relational ties, without compromise, we face a situation beyond our control. So when you have done all that you know to do, there are few alternatives other than to first accept it. It doesn't mean that you like it or agree with it but you are forced to accept it. This is more easily said than done. Most of the time, we don't want to accept it.

We continue to hold on to hope, not realizing that it is false hope. Secondly, before you let go, you must be sure that they really mean what they are saying. You must be convinced that what they are saying is not out of hurt but because they have given it much thought and prayer and believe that it's what's best for them.

It took me a while to let go or to accept the arrival of this point in my life. I'm not saying that she no longer loved me but she no longer felt that being married to me was best for her. I did some things as a result of our growing apart that were not right. For a while, I thought that she was just angry, tired or hurt and felt when she cooled off she would want me back. It took me a while to accept the inevitable. Now mind you, that it did not take me as long as most people because I'm analytical, practical, and the kind of person who will eventually look forward and not backward more quickly than many individuals would. **I am in love with life and want to be happy.**

Because I love life and wanted to be the best person that I could be, I accelerated the healing process. I thank God for the Bible because it taught me this. I also thank God for many years of counseling others. I praise God that just as He had given me words for other hurting people, He also gave me words for my own healing. I also surrounded myself with people who could give me Godly, solid, and unbiased counsel. That being said, months of separation had passed and now months of divorce had passed. She was dating and so was I before I was able to let go. You remember that boy whom I told you about who kissed the house in zero degree temperature; that's how I felt. I had left a part of me behind and she had left a part of herself in my life.

There is even a more difficult aspect of letting go. I hated to even think about this one. Here it is! **Letting go gives the other party the freedom to choose someone else**. Oh no, not another man with my former wife! Well, that was just a fact of life that I had to face. As hard as this may be for you to accept, it is a great possibility. Like me, you must prepare for this to happen. Ready or not, it happened to me and in time I accepted it.

In an earlier chapter, I talked about the first time that I was aware that my ex-wife was dating. I tried to act as if I didn't notice but my heart started racing, and I got a lump in my throat. I felt so sick until I just wanted to get out of the house. Now, as I write this, the initial shock and hurt are long since healed but believe me, it was no laughing matter then.

Did I accept it? You bet I did! Did I let go? You bet I did! I had no choice. This in itself could have driven me crazy. **I could not build a life for myself if I continued to try to monitor hers.** I talk about this because it is very important for you to understand as you go through the process of healing.

How Did I Let Go?

To let go was one of the more difficult things that I have ever had to do. It was a process and came into place after I made a conscious effort to do the following:

1. **I had to come to terms and accept that she really wanted out.** Her wanting out did not make her wrong or a bad person. She just didn't wish to invest any more emotions in us.

2. **I accepted reaching a point of no return.** I realized that if I did go back, the situation was unchanged; we were still on a different plane headed in opposite

directions. I accepted the fact that if I did go back I would not be happy. There are so many people who know that they are not happy in the marriage and they break up and then they go back together only to break up again. The problem was still there, but because of an emotional connection they reconcile but it doesn't last. So, I searched my heart and felt that if I had the opportunity to return, it wouldn't work. I'm not telling you to not keep trying if you feel there is a chance, but even though I was in love with her at that time, deep down inside I knew that it was over.

3. **I put my past marriage and mistakes in God's hands**. I turned it all over to the Lord. I was counseled by a dear friend to release her. It was like she was pulling away, but I in my heart, wouldn't allow her. Let me tell you that's dangerous to you and can cause mental and physical problems. There are many people who have physical problems over failed relationships. I can see why this happens.

4. **I accepted counsel from a godly person to go into my chamber of prayer**, fall on my face and consult

God. How much better our life would be if we would have the first consultation with God. Certainly, we spend countless hours and days seeking the opinions of our peers. I can tell you that there is nothing better than consulting God. I went into my place of prayer in the bedroom in my small apartment. I still remember how I laid prostrate before Him. With tears in my eyes and sorrow and pain in my heart, I asked God if there was a chance of us reconciling and if we did, could we make it. When I prayed to God I told Him that I was not leaving this room until I got an answer. I thought I was going to be in there all day, but God answered me immediately. The answer of course was not what I wanted to hear. I wanted to hear Him say, *"Be patient my child. You will be reconciled. She will come around and you will be together again."*

God did not say that! Instead, I can still hear Him saying to me, "IT'S OVER. Move on with your life and release her. Release her not for her, but release her for YOU. You can't go forward holding on to a dead situation."

Remember God does not override free will. She had made a conscious decision. Her petition was contrary to what I wanted. He honored her privilege of free will. He chose to answer me in another manner.

I did what God told me to do and from that day until now, she has been released from my life and I have had no intentions to ever return. I don't say this from bitterness but that's how strongly I believe in doing what God tells me to do. I would encourage you to do the same thing. If He tells you to hold on, DO IT! If He tells you to let go, DO IT! I did it and my life has been tremendously blessed.

5. **I went into prayer again but this time not for me but for her.** I prayed for her happiness and her success in life. The marriage is over. I acknowledged some things that I'm not proud of. I had caused hurt in her life and now I prayed for healing in her life. I needed to release her and release myself from the torment. **It was only then that complete healing began.**

Remember I shared with you the scar that has been on my leg for thirty-five years as a result of the incident with the cross-cut-saw. Oh I admit that the scars from divorce are still very visible. Scars or THOUGHTS can never be totally erased; but the key is, when healing takes place— they don't hurt anymore. You can heal too! When you allow the healing process to begin and take its course, you will be able to say like me – there is still LIFE AFTER DIVORCE!

Settling the Matter...

I am a grateful and living witness that there is life after divorce. In spite of the many things that I have endured, I have been tremendously blessed to overcome. None of this came without challenges. I believe that there are times when God allows us to encounter setbacks. I also believe that our SETBACKS can be SET-UPS for a COMEBACK! Divorce abruptly injected many setbacks into my life; yet, I am back!

I am back to living my life in happiness and wholeness. God has greatly blessed me. I am a real testimony of how much one can overcome with God. He will help you to make the necessary adjustments in life in order for you to find that peaceful place in your life. He will also stay with you as you go through your valley experience. Remember, David, the psalmist said it like this, *"Yea though I walk*

THROUGH the valley of the shadow of death, I will fear no evil because GOD IS WITH ME!"

I have shared with you the fact that I am remarried and now live my life with a wonderful and loving wife whom I believe God made for me, and by the same token, me for her. It took many years of my life to find her, but God does not operate on our time-table. *His ways are not our ways and His thoughts are not our thoughts.* I believe that if we really want what God has designated for us, then we must enlist patience.

As I complete this book, we have been married for about two and a half years. I want to thank her for patience with me as she has been with me through many things. **Remember, marriage is not the coming together of two persons but the collision of two histories.** When those two histories come together it can present a real need for adjustment. I have a history that she has embraced. Likewise, she has one that I have embraced. That being the case, my lovely wife and I are adjusting and developing a magnificent union.

Challenges are imminent by virtue of the fact that two histories have collided. Moreover, I have now shared my personal saga with the world. This could have presented a greater challenge if we had allowed it. Instead, Tamara was my greatest supporter of this project. She read my manuscript and was very instrumental in making many needed corrections. I'm very sure that some of the content of this book was not comfortable reading for her; however, she was very understanding and helpful as I undertook this assignment given to me by God. I am fortunate that I discussed and disclosed my life story in details prior to marriage. I always feel that it is fair for the person who has pledged to spend the rest of her life with you, to be aware of the intimate details of your life; even if they occurred prior to your coming together.

The early manuscript for this book began to take shape shortly after the finalization of the divorce. I started this as somewhat of a therapeutic journal so that I could chronicle my feelings as I went through the process. I felt led of God to share my story with others after talking with several persons who had similar experiences. From this it turned into the book you have just read. You have had the benefit of an account of the personal and intimate account of special chapters in my life.

You may wonder why I felt the need to divulge this kind of personal information. First of all, I believe that I can help some other person who might feel his or her life is over because of divorce. Secondly, because I believe that if you want life after divorce it will come only after you face the mistakes that occurred in the failed marriage. I'm not the kind of person to just put my head in the sand and act as if nothing has happened. The total experience has changed my life! It has made me better and not bitter. I believe in both the perfect and permissive will of God. Marriage is God's perfect will for a man and woman who desire to enter the most intimate human relationship. When His perfect will does not manifest (the relationship ends) then His permissive will mercifully causes Him to remain by our side. Ultimately, whatever we go through has been ALLOWED by Him.

Somewhat to my surprise, I continued to breathe after divorce. Not only did I want to breathe, I wanted TO LIVE! I WANTED A FULL LIFE! I WANT THE SAME FOR YOU!